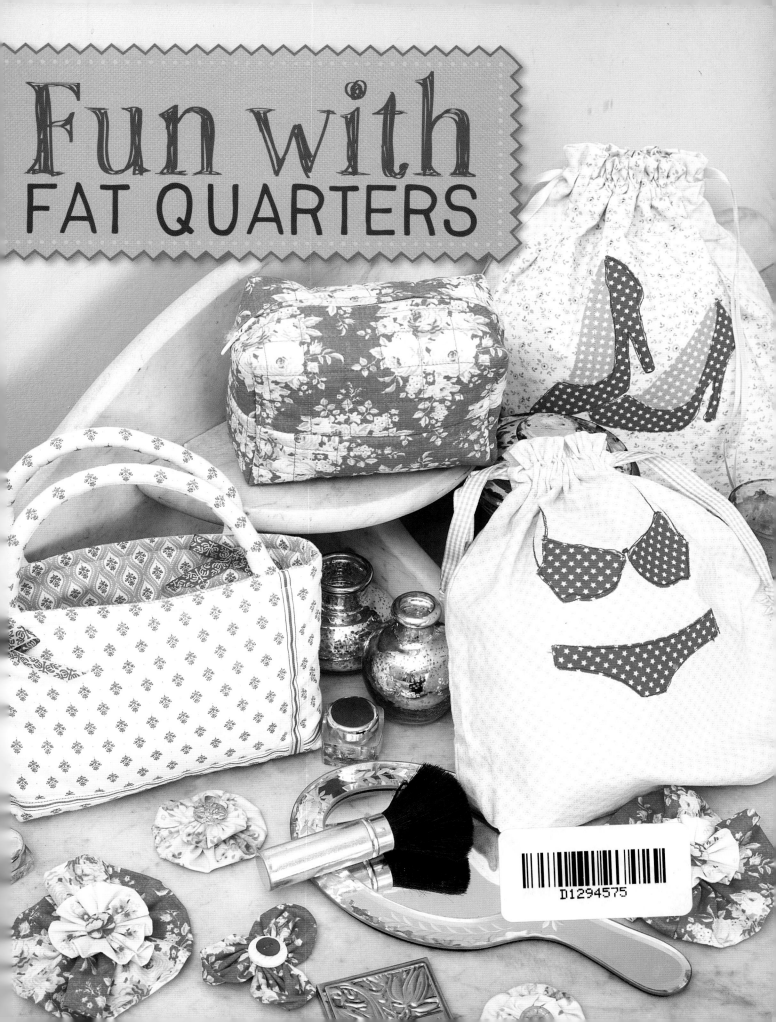

Fun with
FAT QUARTERS

Dedication

This book is dedicated to my family —
my husband Lez, and Jake and Charlie — for
putting up with me sewing at all hours, and to
my fabulous sewing group in Waterlooville
who are always so enthusiastic about
projects I design — they provide
much inspiration.

Fun with
FAT QUARTERS

15 gorgeous sewing projects for using up your fabric stash

WENDY GARDINER

SEARCH PRESS

First published in 2015

Search Press Limited
Wellwood, North Farm Road,
Tunbridge Wells, Kent TN2 3DR

Reprinted 2016, 2017

Photographs by Simon Pask, pages 1–7, 40–93
Photographs by Paul Bricknell, pages 8–39
Illustrations by Jane Smith
Photographs, illustrations and design copyright ©
Search Press Ltd 2015

Text copyright © Wendy Gardiner 2015

ISBN: 978-1-78221-146-4

Suppliers
For details of suppliers, please visit the
Search Press website: www.searchpress.com

Printed in China through Asia Pacific Offset

CONTENTS

Acknowledgements

With many thanks to Groves for the fabulous Tilda fabrics, Hemline haberdashery and Gütermann thread, and to The Cotton Patch for the Amy Butler fabrics. Thanks also to Brother for their sewing machine which made making the projects so much easier, to Vilene for the interfacings, soluble stabilisers and wadding (batting) and of course, thanks to my lovely family — husband Lez and boys Jake and Charlie for supporting me while I burned the midnight oil.

Introduction

I love working with fat quarters. There's such an exquisite range of fabrics to choose from, and their size means that they provide the chance to handle, sew and combine delicious fabric prints in small quantities that you might not otherwise be able to afford, or might not think about putting together. With fat quarters – particularly those that are sold in coordinating bundles – the choice of what to team with what is done for you... leaving you with more time to sew!

So if you have ever been tempted by the wonderful array of fat quarter bundles, or have some that you couldn't resist but don't quite know what to do with, take a look at the range of projects I've put together. Each is made with between one and four fat quarters. They are quick and easy to make but have definite wow factor. To help you get started, I've also included a useful techniques section at the beginning of the book, which will give you guidance for the projects included and will set you up for all your future sewing.

I do hope that you enjoy making these projects and that you shop for fat quarters guilt-free in future – safe in the knowledge that you will be able to make them up into something wonderful.

Happy sewing!

Wendy G

What is a fat quarter?

Quite simply, a fat quarter is a quarter of a metre of fabric. But instead of being cut from selvedge to selvedge, which would result in a long narrow strip measuring 25cm (9¾in) by the width of the fabric, the metre is cut in half vertically and horizontally – like a window pane – so that each quarter square is 'fat'. Fat quarters usually measure about 50 x 45–57cm (19¾ x 17¾–22½in), depending on the width from which the fabric is cut.

Fat quarters are usually 100% cotton or polycotton. They are often sold in coordinating packs, with the range of fabrics carefully selected to work well together. A bundle of fat quarters saves so much time trying to match up fabrics and is an easy way to buy and use small quantities. In this book, I have used fat quarters as the key pieces in projects, and then occasionally added plain or coordinating fabrics for lining and backing.

Tip
A fat quarter will include one selvedge edge, which runs down the lengthwise grain of the fabric. When it is necessary to match grain lines, or to cut a piece on the straight grain, make sure the piece is parallel to the selvedge.

Materials

Arm yourself with a few basic materials to help complete any project. I've selected my must-have materials and a few delicious extras that will add a designer style all of your own.

Fabrics

Gather a selection of fat quarters – look for coordinating packs and you will soon be inspired to sew. Team these with some basic plain or matching fabrics to use for linings and backing fabrics. As most fat quarters are 100% cotton, make sure any additional fabrics are also cotton or polycotton to match.

Threads

Always use good-quality threads that will not shred and break easily. A good selection of colours will ensure you have what you need for each project. Have plenty of black, white and cream and then add in red, pink, green, blue, navy, purple, brown, yellow and orange. Also add a reel of invisible thread to your stash – it's ideal for quilting and 'stitching in the ditch' as it is virtually invisible. It is available in clear or smoky grey.

Trimmings

Ribbon, lace or fringing can lift a project from plain and simple to stunning and unique. When sewing trims, it's easy to ensure they will lie straight if you fuse them in place with hemming web first. Stitch trims over 1cm (½in) wide down both long edges using a thread to match the trim (see page 34).

Interfacings

Interfacing is an additional layer placed on the reverse of a fabric to give it extra body and support. There is a whole range of purpose-made interfacings, available in white or charcoal, in fusible (iron-on) or sew-in varieties, and in light-, medium- or heavy-weight thickness. For craft projects, an iron-on medium-weight interfacing is generally ideal and is available by the metre or in packs.

Hemming web comes in strips that are fusible on both sides and is used to anchor trims in place before you sew them.

Fusible web comes as double-sided sheets of fine glue with a paper backing, and is used to anchor appliqué shapes to a main fabric. Fuse the unprotected side to the reverse of your fabric, draw your design on the paper and then cut out the design. Remove the paper backing to reveal the glue, position and fuse the appliqué to your main fabric.

Wadding (batting) is a thick, fluffy material, usually white or cream, that is sandwiched between the main fabric and a backing or lining fabric, then quilted. It is often used in items such as quilts and bags. Wadding (batting) is available in packs or by the metre, in different thicknesses, in 100% cotton or polyester or in various blends and now even in bamboo.

Tip
To colour match a thread to a fabric, choose a thread colour slightly darker than the fabric, as when it comes off the reel in a single strand, it will appear paler.

Tools

There are lots of different sewing tools, basic equipment and useful gadgets to help create the perfect project and indeed, having the right tool can make a real difference to how easy a project is to sew!

Sewing machine

This will help you make projects quickly and easily and is definitely a must-have. If you are buying a new machine, choose one that can do more than you initially need it for so that as you expand your repertoire of projects, your machine will keep up.

My preference is for a computerised machine because they are so simple to use. Not only will the machine set the stitch length and width to create a perfect stitch every time, it will usually have an LCD window showing the stitch choice, which foot to use and the stitch length and width.

What to look for in a sewing machine

- Easy threading and bobbin winding
- Stitch speed control - so that you can go slowly or more quickly
- A choice of both utility stitches – such as blind hem, overlock, zigzag and triple zigzag – and decorative stitches
- Stitch width and stitch length control, so that you can adjust these to suit different fabrics and projects
- Easy buttonholes (one-step or four-step)
- Twin-needle facility

Machine needles

These need to be changed regularly – after every eight hours of sewing or with every new project – plus, of course, there are different types of needles for use with different fabrics. Keep a selection of universal sharp needles for most woven fabrics in sizes 70–90 (10–14) and a more robust needle for thicker fabrics or multi-layers, in size 100 (16). For stretchy fabrics you will need some ball-point and stretch needles, while twin needles create two perfectly parallel rows at the same time (see page 32).

Hand needles

A good selection of hand needles is always useful. They are great for finishing off projects, taking thread tails to the back and slip stitching turning gaps closed.

Pins

Good-quality, sharp pins are a must and, like needles, they do need replacing occasionally as they blunt over time and will snag fabrics. Those with coloured glass heads are useful as they are easy to handle and remove as you sew and, of course, can be seen more easily when dropped!

Tip

Place pins at right angles in the work so you can remove them as you sew.

Seam ripper

Also known as a 'quick unpick', this is a very useful tool for accurately removing stitches. Most sewing machines will come with a seam ripper, but they do blunt over time, so invest in a new one if you are starting to find it difficult to slice through thread or open buttonholes.

Steam iron

This is an essential aid to sewing, as every seam should be pressed before you stitch over it again. Ironing your seams embeds the stitching and presses them nice and flat. Use a pressing cloth to protect the fabric and work with a hotter iron than the fabric can withstand alone – a square of cotton or silk organza makes an ideal pressing cloth as it is transparent and can withstand high temperatures.

Point turner

This useful gadget has a point at one end and is used to help turn out corners properly. Many types have measurements along one side and some even have a button gauge: a shaped opening that can be useful when machine sewing buttons in place. To use it, position the opening of the point turner under the button's holes so that when you stitch through the button it is slightly raised away from the fabric – this will create a thread shank as you sew. To finish, wrap the thread around the shank a few times before securing the thread end.

Bias-binding maker

This nifty gadget allows you to create bias binding from any fabric you like, rather than relying on types available to buy. You feed strips of bias-cut fabric through it, and as they pull through, the long edges are folded to the centre, creating neat, folded binding strips. It's best to work on an ironing board and iron the creases in place as you go. Bias binding makers come in different sizes to create different widths of binding. A good starting point is a 2.5cm (1in) maker.

Self-covered buttons

A pack of these in your workbox will ensure you can finish a project that needs a button without having to scour the shops for a good match.

Needle grabbers

Needle grabbers make it easier to pull a hand needle through thick layers of fabric easily.

Non-slip matting

Non-slip matting really helps you to keep control over your fabric when you are free-motion stitching on the sewing machine. Place a couple of little patches of it under your fingers as you guide the fabric (see page 25). You can also buy special quilting gloves with non-slip pads on the fingers.

Needle threader

This is a real boon when sewing in low light. This gadget has a very fine wire loop that is passed through the eye of the needle. You insert the thread through the loop before pulling it and the thread back through the needle eye. These are also useful if sewing with thicker threads.

Tape measure

A good-quality tape measure, with both imperial and metric measurements, is essential. Just make sure that you follow either metric or imperial for each project – do not try to mix them, particularly when patchworking or quilting, where precision is necessary. Do replace a tape measure that is very old as over time they can stretch and thus not be accurate.

Hem gauge

This is a small gadget useful for marking up hems. Many also have a little hole in either end so that you can use them to draw perfect circles – put a pin in one end to mark the circle centre and a pen in the other to draw the shape.

Acrylic ruler, rotary cutter and mat

If you are going to do any patchwork and quilting, an acrylic ruler, rotary cutter and cutting mat is a trio of must-haves. The acrylic rulers are clear, with distinct measurements along the edges and grid lines that can be matched up with straight edges on fabric and the cutting mat. Some also have angled lines so that you can easily cut fabrics on the bias. A rotary cutter has a circular blade and is used in conjunction with an acrylic ruler and cutting mat to cut straight edges on fabric quickly and accurately. You can also cut multiple layers at one time. Slightly angle the cutter so that the blade is against the ruler and push it away from you. Cutting mats have grids in either imperial or metric measurements – often one type of measurement on each side – and are usually 'self-healing', which means they can be used time and time again. Line up the fabric with the grid on the mat and the grid on the acrylic ruler to ensure perfectly straight edges.

Dressmaking scissors

These are absolutely essential for cutting fabric. They often have moulded handles that are easier on the hand, particularly with repeated use, with blades angled from the handle so they cut along the table smoothly. If you are left-handed, look for left-handed shears, as the moulded handles will be uncomfortable if designed for right-handed use.

Pinking shears

While not essential, these are really handy as they make light work of neatening the raw edges of lightweight fabrics such as cottons, felts and linen-like fabrics. The jagged blades cut the fabric with a zigzag edge to prevent fraying.

Embroidery scissors

These are very useful for snipping thread ends and clipping into small areas – keep a pair of sharp embroidery scissors in your workbox.

Marking pencils, pens and chalk

Have a selection of marking options available to suit different fabrics and jobs. For instance, disappearing (fade-away) pens are ideal for temporarily marking darts and pocket placements. Other soluble pens will wash away, while chalk pencils or chalk wheels leave a mark that can be brushed away.

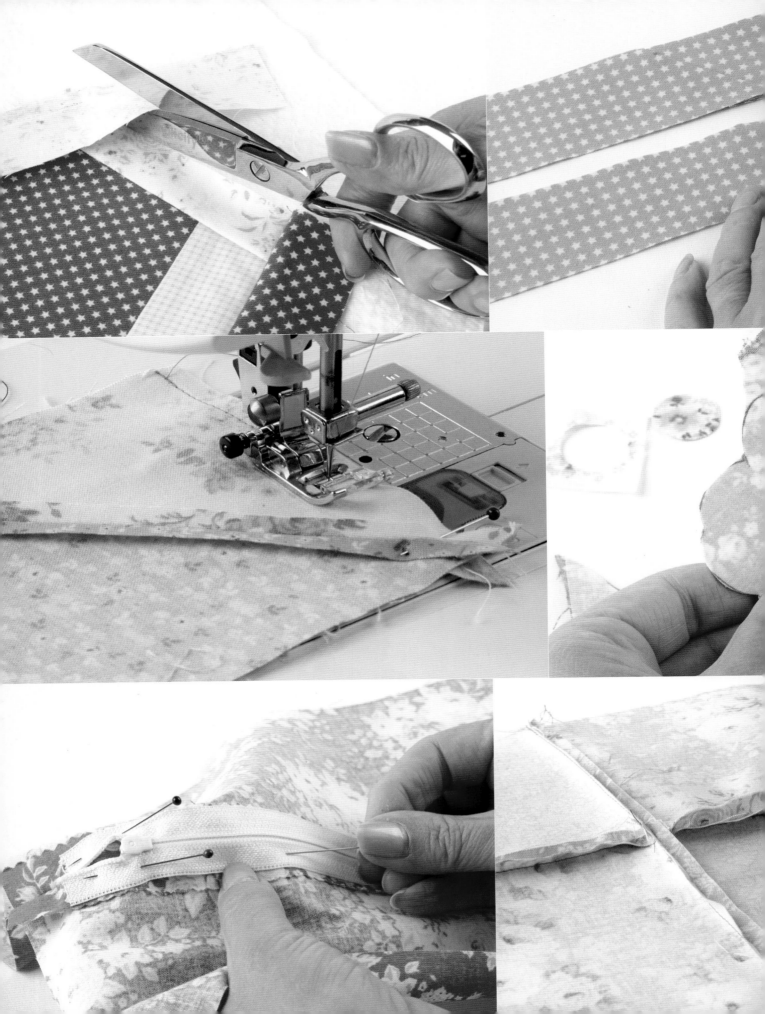

Techniques

This chapter includes lots of useful techniques to help you make the projects in this book, and which will also be useful for your future makes. All are easily explained with step-by-step photography, guiding you through the process so that before you know it you will have mastered various seams and finishes, different patchwork and quilting techniques, zip insertion, decorative stitching and more specialist techniques such as piping, appliqué and free-motion stitching.

Seaming

A seam is used to join two layers of fabric together and is generally sewn with a straight stitch with right sides of fabric together. The gap between the seam stitching and the fabric edge is called the seam allowance.

Tip

Use the edge of the presser foot as a guide to sew a straight line. Alternatively, draw a stitching guideline using disappearing marking pen.

Simple seam

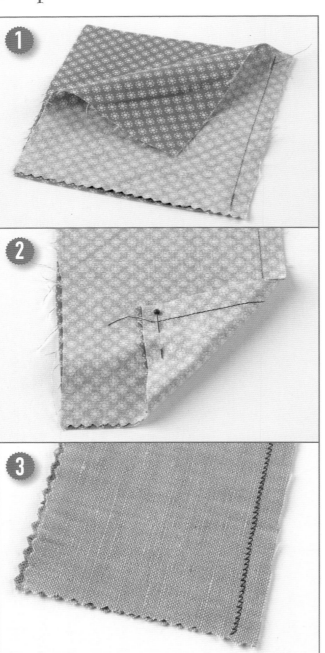

1 Position your pieces of fabric, pinned right sides together, under the sewing machine foot so that the needle will fall into the fabric approximately 15mm (⁵⁄₈in) from the end and 6mm (¼in) in from the right raw edges. Note that for dressmaking, the needle should usually fall about 15mm (⁵⁄₈in) from the raw edges.

2 Stitch forward two or three stitches then, holding the reverse button on your sewing machine, stitch backwards to the fabric edge. Let go of the reverse button to stitch forwards again. At the end of the seam, repeat the reverse stitching to anchor the thread.

3 For stretchy fabrics, sew the seam with a stretch stitch or very small zigzag stitch. A stretch stitch looks like a small, slanted zigzag or like three parallel straight stitches. To set the zigzag stitch for a stretch seam, reduce the stitch width to 2 and the length to 1.

French seam

This neatly encases the raw edge of the seam allowance.

1 First, sew the fabric wrong sides together taking a 6mm (¼in) seam. Trim the seam allowance to about 3mm (⅛in).

2 Refold the fabric right sides together and press with the seam on the edge of the fabric. Sew the seam again, with a 6mm (¼in) seam. The raw edges are now neatly encased within the seam, as shown. Press again.

How to finish your seams

1. Once the seam is stitched, press. Then select a zigzag stitch, increase the length to 2 and stitch along the seam allowance only. If you are working on lightweight fabrics you can sew both seam allowances together; if the fabric is medium- or heavy-weight, press the seam allowances open and stitch down each individually.

2. For transparent or silky fabrics, sew a seam, then a small zigzag stitch right next to the seam. Trim the seam allowance close to the zigzag stitching.

3. For lightweight cottons and felt, use pinking shears to neaten the raw edge of the seam allowance.

4. After sewing the seam, overedge stitch the seam allowance raw edges using an overedge foot and stitch. The foot has a deeper right toe which protrudes below the left toe and a metal pin in the needle aperture. Butt the fabric edge against the inner edge of the protruding toe. The overedge stitch has a straight stitch to the left with a zigzag stitch to the right – the zigzag stitches sit right on the edge of the fabric, over the metal pin that is holding the fabric flat.

Patchworking

Cutting fabric into pieces and joining it together again in a chosen design is called 'patchworking'. It is a great way to use small pieces of favourite fabrics or to create eye-catching projects from mixed fabric pieces.

Tip

Always pin the pieces together at the seams first in order that you perfectly match the seam joins, and then pin to the outer edges.

Simple square patches

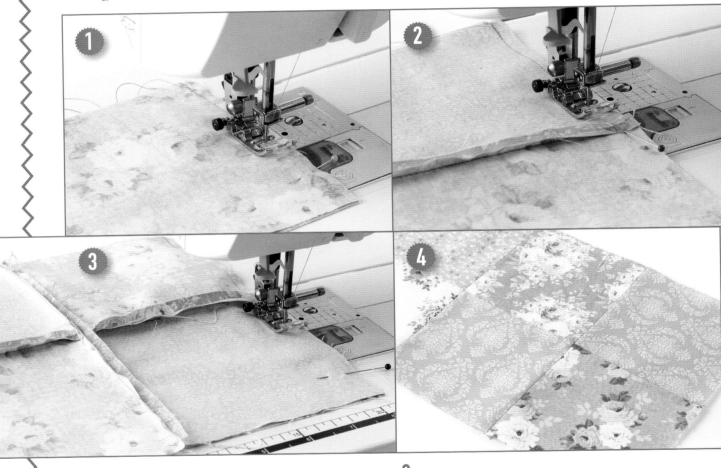

1 Cut two equal-sized squares of fabric. Pin them, right sides together, then sew with a 6mm (¼in) seam.

3 Now open out the four-patch and pin to another four-patch, again matching and pinning the centre seam first, then pinning the outer edges. Sew together.

2 Open out the two-patch piece and join to another two-patch piece, first matching the centre seam together, then the outer edges. Again sew with a 6mm (¼in) seam.

4 Press all the seams – either press seam allowances open or towards the darker patch. Continue to join squares together in this manner until you reach your desired size.

Half-square triangles: pinwheel patchwork

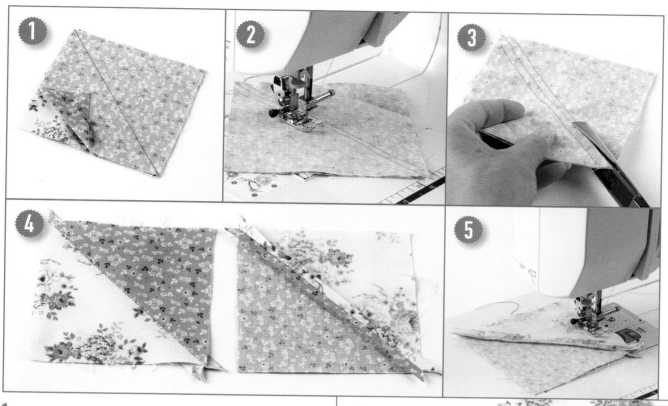

1 Cut two squares each of fabric from two coordinating fat quarters. Place two contrast pieces, right sides together and draw a diagonal line down the centre.

2 Taking a 6mm (¼in) seam allowance, stitch down each side of the drawn line.

3 Cut along the drawn line, cutting both fabric layers at the same time. Repeat steps 1–3 for the second pair of coordinating squares.

4 Open out the new fabric pieces, which will have two contrast triangles in each piece. Press the seam allowances open.

Tip

Sew the seams until the last 6mm (¼in), then stop and anchor the stitching. This will make the centre easier to join where all the seams come together.

5 Take two of the patches, turn one by one rotation, to create the pin wheel effect, and then sew them right sides together along one edge. Repeat for the second pair of patches.

6 With right sides together, pin the two sets of patches together, making sure you match the centre where the seams join. Sew and press.

Stitch-and-flip crazy patchwork

1 Cut a five-sided crazy patch – you can use a template or cut the shape to your own chosen size. Pin the patch, right side up, in the centre of a square of wadding (batting) or backing fabric that is approximately three times the height and width of your patch. Cut fabric strips from three or four contrast fabrics, about 2.5–5cm (1–2in) wide. Place one small strip, right side down on top of the crazy patch, so that the right edge is in line with the edge of the patch. Stitch in place taking a 6mm (¼in) seam.

2 Open out the first strip and then add a second strip facing right side down – it should run along the next crazy-patch edge and extend up to the end of your first strip. Stitch in place taking a 6mm (¼in) seam.

3 Flip the second strip open and place a third contrast strip along the third side of the crazy patch.

4 As you flip the strips over, trim off excess length for use later.

5 Continue in this manner around the crazy patch until you have covered the backing fabric.

6 Press the complete patch and then turn it over and trim the lapping strips back to the size of the backing fabric. The panel is now ready to be used as a pillow front or centre of a table runner.

Tip
Cut the strips in varying widths from 2.5–5cm (1–2in) to create a truly 'crazy' panel.

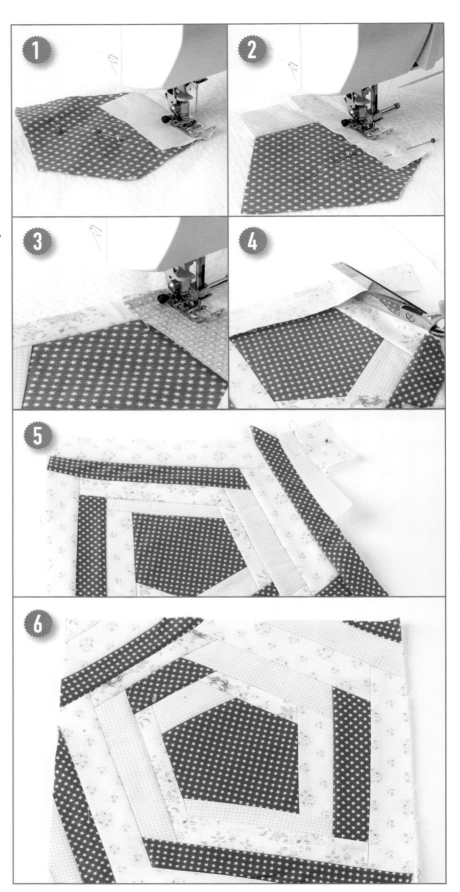

Further patchwork inspiration

1. Half-square triangles cut from two complementary fabrics have been sewn together to create a lovely spiral pinwheel.

2. Create a disappearing nine-patch design by first sewing a nine-patch, then cutting vertically and horizontally through the centre patches. Turn the top right and bottom left pieces by one rotation. Then sew top-right and bottom-right pieces together and sew top-left and bottom-left pieces together. Finally sew right to left (see page 77).

3. Start with a simple square and add one border, flip open and then add the next border as for the stitch-and-flip method. Continue in this manner, working your way clockwise around the edges, until the size required is achieved.

4. Stitch decorative stitches across a plain fabric and then cut it with a crazy-patch template. Add the strips around the edges (as on page 22) and then over-stitch with some decorative stitches using bright contrast thread.

5. Make a simple nine-patch piece using three squares each from three coordinating fabrics. Sew them together in a strip of three, making sure each of the fabrics is in a left, central and right position. Then sew the three strips together.

6. Join strips together diagonally. Start with the first strip right side up diagonally across the centre of a backing fabric. Lay the second strip, right side down on top of the first with right side edges together. Sew, flip and continue adding strips. Repeat for the other side edge of the centre strip until the backing fabric is completely covered (see page 26).

Quilting

Anchoring layers of fabric together with stitch, usually when they have a layer of wadding (batting) between them, is known as 'quilting'. Patchwork and quilting go hand in hand. You can quilt by hand or using your machine, and it's important to select your stitch and style so that it suits your project.

Straight lines

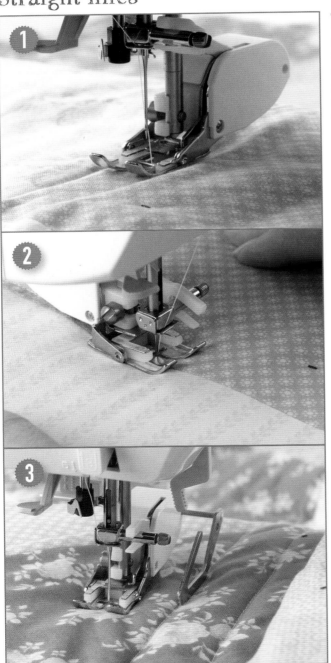

1 The easiest method of quilting is in straight lines, with a straight stitch. Pin baste (tack) or hand baste (tack) the layers together, starting at the centre and working out towards the edge. Then attach a walking foot to help feed the layers of fabric through the machine evenly and smoothly.

Check

Make sure when attaching the walking foot that the bar on the right of the foot is positioned over the top of the needle bar. Increase the stitch length to 2.8–3.

2 Stitch in the ditch of the seam joins, gently pulling the fabric apart as you sew. Use invisible thread in the top if you want to make the stitching virtually invisible. Increase the tension to approximately 7–8 so that the bobbin thread is not visible on the top.

3 Use a quilting guide to keep your parallel lines evenly spaced – insert it in the back of the walking foot and sew repeated parallel lines across the quilt top. You can push the guide in or out to create the desired distance between rows of stitching. Sew the first row and then move the guide in or out by the desired amount so that the guide will run along the previous row of stitching. Approximately 2.5–4cm (1–1½in) apart is an attractive gap. Continue stitching parallel lines across the quilt. If desired, turn the work and repeat to create a grid.

Tip

If working on a small patch, you can sew a grid diagonally, starting across the centre, to create a diamond-stitched grid.

Free-motion quilting

1 Set up the machine for free-motion stitching: drop the feed dogs (check your manual if necessary), set the stitch length to zero and attach a darning or free-motion foot. Thread the machine with a thread colour to either tone with the fabric top or contrast with it.

2 Holding the fabric flat, lower the presser foot – it will not sit firmly on the fabric as other feet do, rather it hovers above. Then with your foot firmly down on the foot pedal start moving the fabric in any direction you like: keep your foot down and move the fabric slowly.

3 Stitch around fabric shapes, and add swirls or a 'meandering' stippling stitch – a curvy line of stitching that wanders across the fabric.

4 Move the fabric in any direction so that you completely cover the surface.

Tips

1. Place backing fabric under the wadding (batting) to help the layers feed smoothly.

2. Use small patches of non-slip matting beneath your fingers, as shown, to help you move and control the direction of the fabric.

3. If you're a little nervous about getting your fingers close to the stitching, secure the fabric in a wooden embroidery hoop and then hold the hoop by the edges.

4. Put your foot down so the motor is going fast but move the fabric at a slow, even pace. The slower and smaller the movement, the smaller the stitch will be; the quicker and faster the movement of fabric, the longer and larger the stitches will be.

5. Check the back of the work and adjust the tension if needed.

6. Try out free-motion stitching on odd fabric scraps to gain confidence.

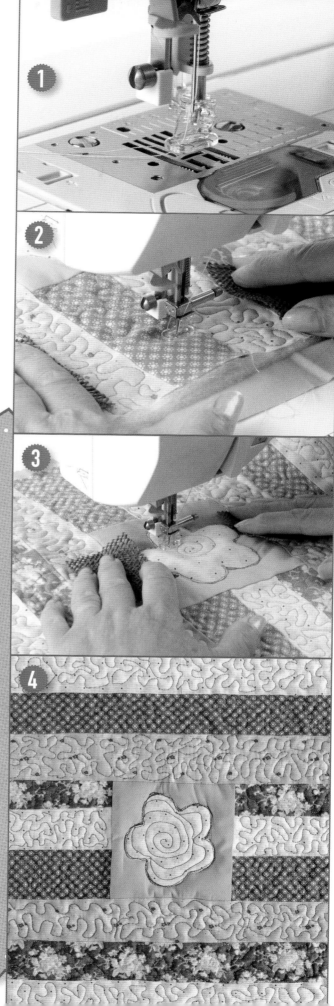

Quilt as you go

This is a variation of the stitch-and-flip patchwork method (see page 22).

1 Lay the backing fabric right side down, then add a layer of wadding (batting). Start with the first strip, placed diagonally across the wadding (batting) right side up. Top with another strip, right side down, matching the right fabric edges. Sew the strips in place through all layers along one edge.

2 Open out the strips and then place a third on top, right side down, with the fabric edges matching. Again stitch in place along one edge. Open out this third strip.

3 Continue to cover the surface with strips in the same way, flipping them over after they are stitched, until the whole background is covered.

4 Trim the panel down to the required size and press. The panel is now ready to be added to a table runner, or used as bag front.

Tip

Cut strips of different widths from remnants left over from other projects.

Further quilting inspiration

1. Use a twin needle and quilter's guide to stitch perfectly parallel rows of quilting in a grid formation. You can use a different thread in each needle, as shown. For more on twin needles see page 32.

2. Use free-motion embroiderery to outline and add detail to an appliqué shape – stitch around the edges three or four times in a 'naive', sketchy manner using a matching thread colour to create this shabby chic look.

3. Stitch a spiral on a plain base to create a visual interest. This can be done with free-motion stitching or regular machine sewing, stopping with needle down and pivoting the fabric as you spiral out.

4. Having joined straight strips, machine quilt them together, sewing 6mm–1cm (¼–½in) away from the seams to create definition and texture.

5. Mirror a particular fabric design by machine stitching around shapes in the fabric print using free-motion stitching.

Adding a zip

Zips add the finishing touch to so many projects, ranging from bags to pillow covers and of course clothes. A centred zip is the easiest to master, with just six simple steps.

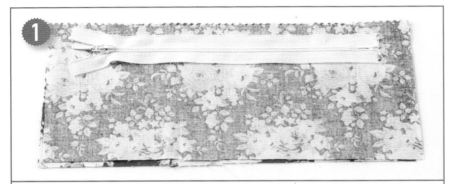

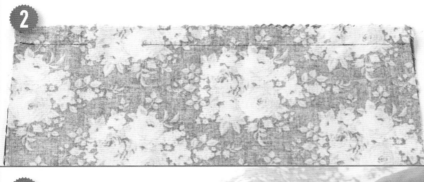

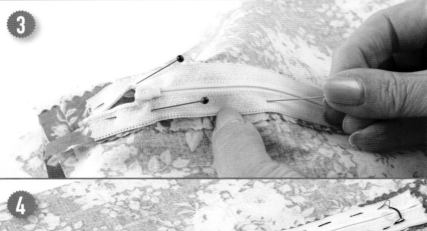

1 Neaten the raw edges of the fabric the zip is to be inserted into, either by pinking with pinking shears or sewing a line of zigzag stitching. Mark the zip position by laying the zip on the wrong side of the fabric and marking the fabric at the top of the zip pull and at the bottom of the teeth.

2 Remove the zip and machine stitch down to the first mark and then backstitch to anchor the stitching. Cut the threads. Increase stitch length to the longest available and, leaving a 3–5cm (1¼–2in) gap, machine baste (tack) down to the second mark. Decrease the stitch length to 2.2–2.5 before stitching the remainder of the seam. Remember to backstitch at the start and end of the regular stitching to anchor the threads.

3 Press the seam allowance open. Lay the zip, face down, on top of the seam with the teeth centered over the seam and the zip pull at the end with the 3–5cm (1¼–2in) gap. Pin in place.

4 With a contrast thread colour machine or hand baste (tack) the zip in position, through all the layers of fabric. Create straight lines down the sides of the zip tape and across the top and bottom.

5 Attach your zip foot. With the zip and fabric right side up, start at the seam at the bottom of the zip. At right angles to the zip seam, take three or four stitches, stop with the needle down, raise the presser foot and swivel the fabric so that you can stitch up the side of the zip, following your basting (tacking) stitches. When you get close to the zip pull, stop with the needle down, raise the presser foot and pull the zip pull down, out of the way. Continue to stitch to the top, pivot and stitch to the seam. Repeat for the other side of the zip.

6 Using a quick unpick, or seam ripper, carefully remove all the hand and machine basting (tacking) stitches, then carefully press the zip.

The finished zip.

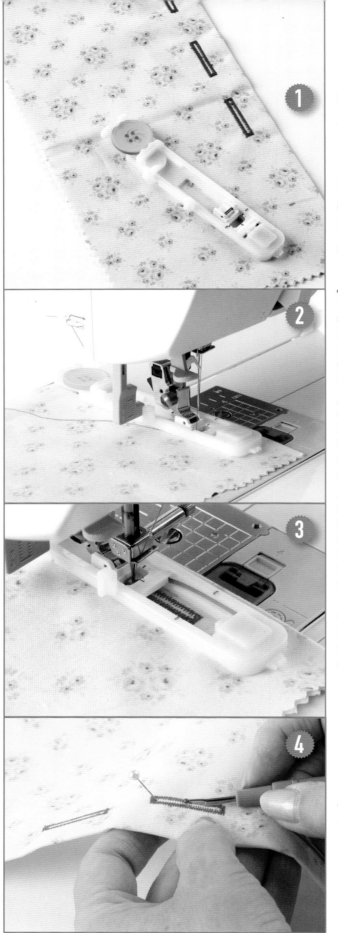

Creating buttonholes

Buttonholes are very easy to sew nowadays as so many machines come armed with nifty buttonhole feet. Each buttonhole stitched should be the perfect size for the button.

1 Mark the buttonhole start position on the fabric, making sure that the holes will be at least 1cm (½in) from the fabric edge (I have marked mine with a dab of fade-away blue pen). Place the button in the back of the foot by pushing away the lever on the left of the foot to open out the holder. Bring the lever back to hold the button securely.

2 Attach the foot to the sewing machine as usual, lining up the bar on the foot with the groove on the foot holder. Bring down the buttonhole guide – from the underside of the left side of the sewing machine. This butts up against the front protruding guide on the foot.

3 Select your buttonhole stitch and position the fabric under the foot so that the marked start line on the fabric is in line with the front markings on the foot. Note that most buttonholes will stitch from the front of the buttonhole backwards towards the back. Let the machine stitch the buttonhole in one step. Take the threads to the back and tie off.

4 To open the buttonhole, place a pin at one end, just inside the bar tack, and then using a quick unpick, or seam ripper, start at the other end and push the blade towards the pin. Trim off any stray fabric threads.

Tip

Some basic machines stitch a four-step buttonhole, so you may need to mark both the start and finish of the buttonhole. Once the first side is stitched, change the stitch selection dial to stitch the bar tack four or five stitches, then change it for the second side, before bar tacking again.

Creating button loops

Another method of fastening buttons is to create little button loops from fabric strips. These thin strips are known as rouleau loops, and can be used to create button loops that look great on pillow covers and bags as well as straps for lightweight garments such as camisoles.

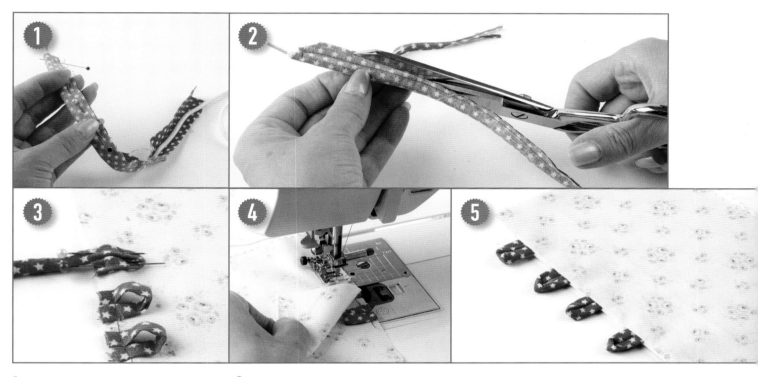

1 Cut a strip of fabric 3cm (1¼in) wide by the length needed. Fold the fabric right sides together lengthways and press. Insert a shoelace into the fold and pin. The shoelace is simply used to turn the fabric strip easily.

2 Stitch across the end of the fabric, catching the shoelace. With the needle down, raise the presser foot and pivot the fabric to sew along the length of the fabric – sew close to the shoelace but do not catch it in your stitching. Trim the seam allowance to a scant 3mm (¹⁄₈in). Pull on the unattached end of the shoelace to pull the strip through to the right side. Carefully unpick the end holding the shoelace before removing it.

3 Cut and fold the strip into 'U'-shaped loops, making them large enough to slip your chosen button through and have a seam allowance of 6mm (¼in). Pin to the right side of the fabric, with the loop towards the fabric and the ends in line with the fabric edge. Baste (tack) in place.

4 Add the second fabric piece or facing, right sides together, sandwiching the loops between the layers. Stitch with a 6mm (¼in) seam.

5 Turn the fabric so that the right sides are facing outwards, revealing the button loops. Press with the seam on the very edge. If desired, top-stitch 3mm (¹⁄₈in) from the edge to hold the facing in place.

Using twin needles

Twin needles create two perfectly parallel rows of stitching at the same time and can add definite wow factor to your projects very easily! They can be used on most sewing machines and are attached in the same manner as single needles. Most sewing-machine manuals will have a stitch guide showing which decorative stitches can be used with a twin needle.

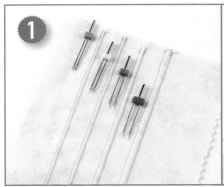 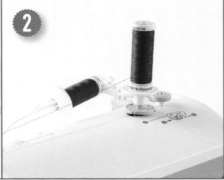 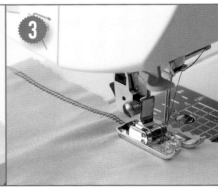

1 Select your needles. Twin needles have two needles attached to one shank and are available in universal sharp, ball-point, stretch and embroidery varieties to sew all sorts of fabrics. They are also available with different gaps between the needles, ranging from 1.6mm (^{1}/$_{16}$in) to 4mm (^{1}/$_8$in).

2 Attach the second thread spindle to your machine – this may be attached to a dedicated hole in the top of the machine, or slipped on to the bobbin winder. Thread the upper threads together until you get to the last guide just above the needle. If possible, slip the left thread behind the guide to the left and the right thread behind the guide to the right. If you only have one guide, leave one thread out of this last guide.

3 Sew a straight stitch and see two perfectly parallel rows appear. The underside will look like a zigzag stitch, as the one bobbin thread is picked up between the two top threads. Now try other stitches, such as zigzag.

Further examples

1. Make pretty dainty pin tucks with a twin needle. Choose one with a gap of 2–3mm (about ^{1}/$_8$in), increase the top tension to the highest (7–9) and sew. As you stitch, the fabric slightly bunches between the two parallel rows as the bobbin thread pulls them together. This becomes more noticeable when you sew several rows close together.

2. Try using two different top-thread colours. Two perfectly parallel rows are stitched together. Check that both needles will go through the presser foot and throat plate without hitting the sides – turn the balance wheel on the right of the machine by hand to lower and raise the needle through the complete stitch pattern to check.

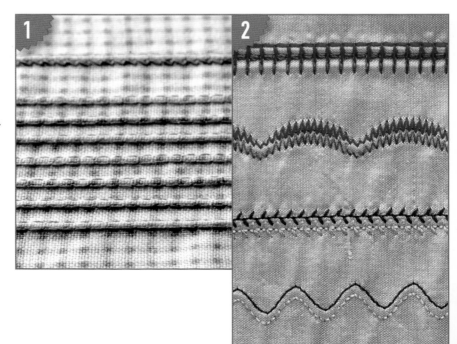

Decorative stitching

I love to embellish and customise products with decorative stitching, particularly using bold contrast threads. A plain fabric pillow cover or economy bedlinen can be enhanced quickly with just a few rows of pretty stitching.

1. Try a variegated thread and stitch some of the concentrated stitch patterns. See how the thread colour change enhances the stitch.

2. Try metallic thread for decorative stitches. Use a metallic needle with metallic threads as the thread can wear a groove in the eye of the needle otherwise, which will cause the thread to shred and snap. Also, stitch a little slower with metallic threads. The results are worth it!

3. Try out the decorative stitches on your machine, using different thread colours. Note that you should back the fabric with interfacing or a tear-away stabiliser when stitching concentrated stitch patterns, as you might otherwise pucker the fabric.

4. Try adjusting the length and width of the stitches to see how they change. Make a note of any changes you like. For instance, a simple zigzag stitch (second down in the picture) becomes a satin stitch when the length is decreased to 0.34–0.40.

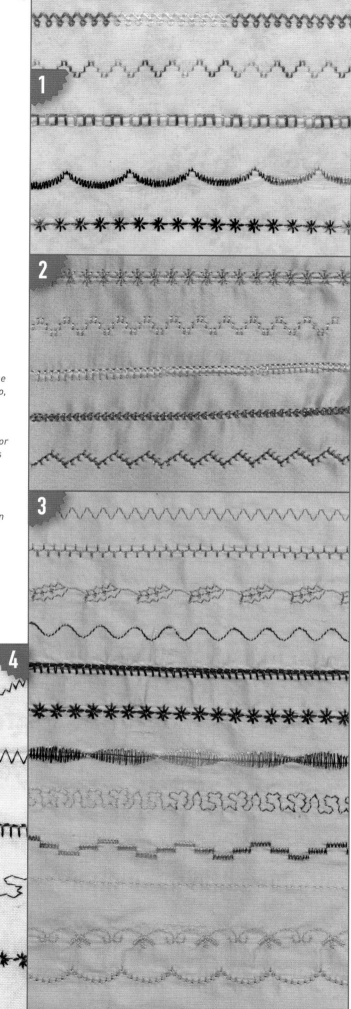

Adding trims

Adding trims is a quick and easy way of upgrading a simple project to something really special. Add ribbon or lace, or couch down a thick thread to give your bag, pillow cover or table runner textural interest.

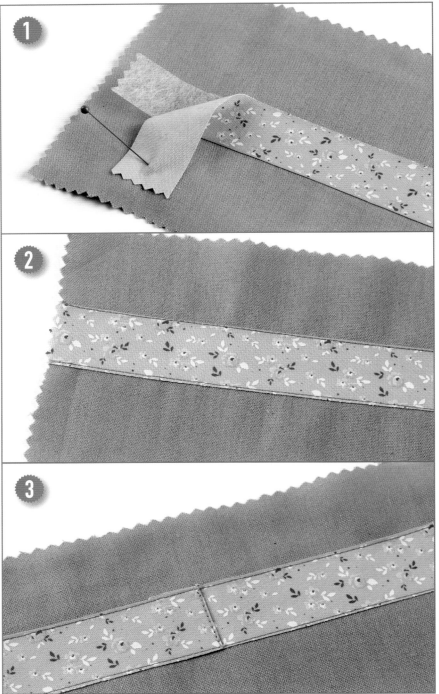

1 To ensure the trim is stitched in a straight line, secure it in place with a strip of hemming web. First, mark the position for the trim, then cut the webbing slightly narrower than this. Place the webbing along the marked line and place the trim on top. Use a hot iron to fuse in place.

2 Stitch trims over 1cm (½in) wide down both sides, sewing both in the same direction, as this will prevent the trim from twisting or rippling. Use a thread colour to match the trim closely. For trims under 1cm (½in), you could stitch down the centre with a wide zigzag or stitch down one edge only, allowing the other to remain free.

3 To join the ends of the trim, tuck the end of the trim under and then overlap the start. Continue to stitch the lapped section in place along the edges. Finish by stitching vertically at the join – you can do this by machine or hand.

Tip

Use a ribbon to create a casing for a drawstring. Stitch it in place along the top and bottom edges as above, leaving a 2cm (¾in) gap on the lower edge to feed in the cord.

Further trim inspiration

1. Attach narrow trims with a triple zigzag stitch. Adjust the stitch width so that it is slightly wider than the trim, and as it stitches, it will stitch either side and in the centre of the trim, anchoring it in place. Couch (stitch) down thicker yarns such as crochet or knitting yarns in the same manner, using a cording foot if available. Alternatively, stitch with a zigzag either side of a piece of narrow ribbon and then pull up some excess to tie little bows.

2. Use decorative stitches to anchor trims in place. Blanket stitching along the edges to create little sideways stitches into the trim looks nice, as does contrast thread stipple stitch or flower stitch.

3. Add lace trims by stitching down the straight edge only using a thread colour to match the lace.

4. A lace insertion is a pretty way to attach decorative lace. First position the lace panel on the fabric and sew around the edge with a thread colour to match the lace. From the underside, carefully cut away the fabric, leaving a 6mm (¼in) seam allowance. Snip into this allowance at curves and corners and then fold it back upon itself away from the lace. Press, baste (tack) and then machine stitch again, working from the right side, to hold the seam allowance in place. The result is a lovely lacy window.

5. Fringing and bobble trims can be attached to the surface, within a seam or along a hem edge. Use a zip foot to attach a bobble trim so that you can sew close to the trim edge without the bobbles getting caught.

6. Add a group of overlapping trims, stitching each down both sides. They can be attached with a thread colour to match the trims, or stitched with a bolder decorative stitch to enhance the combination.

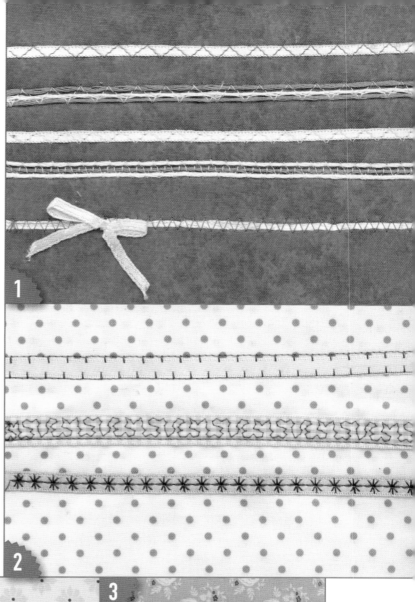

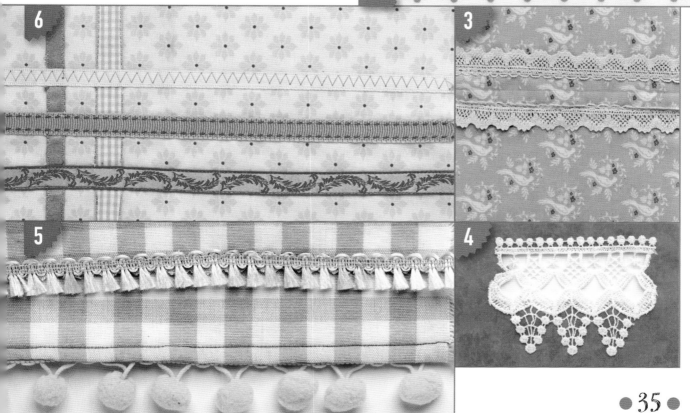

Adding piping

Piping adds a professional finish to so many projects and provides a crisp, clean edging. Piping can be bought ready-made with a fabric flap for attaching it, or can be made from your own fabric to create a perfect match or contrast for your project.

1 Piping is made from bias strips of fabric. To cut several strips, first draw parallel lines 4–5cm (1½–2in) wide diagonally across a strip of fabric. To find the bias, fold the cut edge of the fabric up towards the selvedge and press. The diagonal crease created is the true bias.

2 To join strips into one long piece, place two ends right sides together at right angles, Stitch across the overlapping fabric from the top-left to bottom-right edge. Cut off the excess corner and fold out the strip. Press.

3 Fold the fabric strip in half, wrong sides together, and press. Insert the piping cord within the strip, pushing it in towards the fold. Stitch down the long edge to anchor the cord in place, starting 5cm (2in) from the end of the fabric.

4 Tuck the raw edge of the unstitched end to the inside and pin the piping to the right side of the project (here I am adding piping to the edge of a pillow cover), starting midway down one side. Attach a zip foot so that the toe of the foot is to the right – away from the piping cord – and start stitching, about 5cm (2in) from the end of the cord.

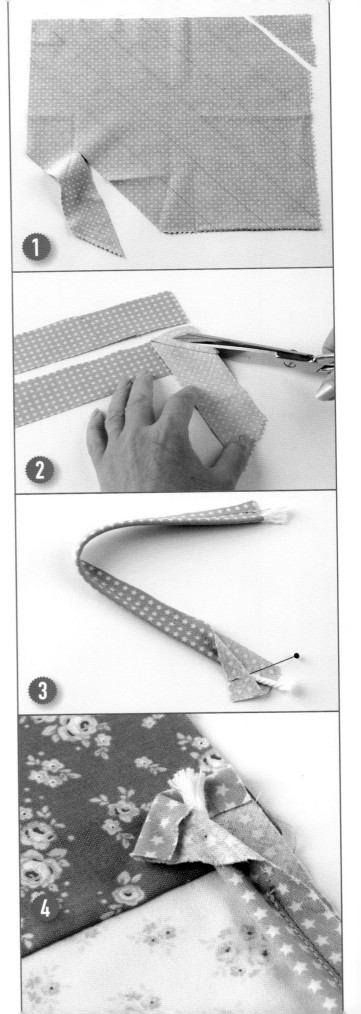

5 When you reach the corner, stop with the needle down, raise the presser foot and snip into the piping fabric only – not the pillow cover – so that it will spread out. Pivot the fabric, take one or two stitches on the corner, stop with the needle down, pivot the fabric again and continue stitching the piping in place along the second edge.

6 Repeat step 5 when you come to the next three corners. When you reach the first side again, stop about 5cm (2in) from the end with the needle down. Raise the presser foot and then open out the beginning of the piping to lay the end inside. Trim the actual cord ends so that they meet, then lap the fabric back over. Continue to stitch until you reach the start of the piping stitching.

7 To finish, place the second layer of fabric, which will form the other side of your pillow cover, on top of the first, right sides together, sandwiching the piping in between the layers. Pin in place all the way round, with the pins placed at right angles so they are easy to remove as you sew.

8 Turn the work over so you can see the stitching holding the piping in position. The aim is now to stitch the fabric pieces together, stitching very, very close to the actual bump of the piping cord and to the left of the previous stitching. If possible, move the needle position to the left so it will stitch right on the edge of the cord. Leave a turning gap along one of the sides.

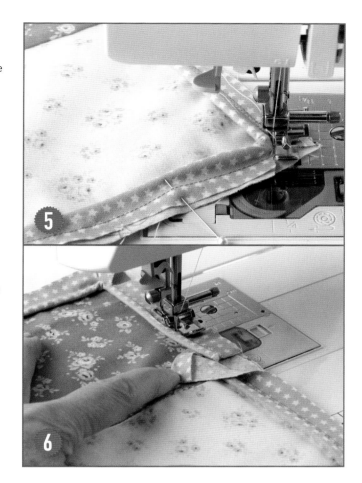

Tip

Don't be frightened by piping. If you haven't stitched it closely enough when encasing the piping, simply stitch again to the left of previous stitching so it is really snug.

9 Turn the cover through to the right side, stuff it, then sew the turning gap closed. Enjoy your professional-looking piping!

Appliqué

An appliqué is an additional motif or fabric design added to the surface of a base fabric. Ready-made appliqué shapes can simply be stitched on, or you can design and make your own.

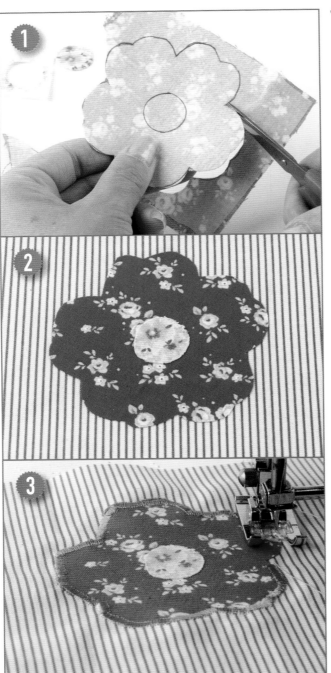

1 Fuse a piece of paper-backed double-sided fusible web to the reverse of your appliqué fabric. Draw around a template or draw your own shape on the paper backing and then cut it out neatly.

2 Peel off the paper backing and then place the design on the base fabric in the desired position. Fuse in place with a hot iron, protecting the fabrics with a pressing cloth.

3 Select a stitch to sew around the appliqué shape. For most fabric appliqué shapes, a satin stitch is ideal – this is a zigzag stitch, changed so that the stitch width is 3mm (⅛in) and the stitch length is reduced to 0.35–0.40 – this closes up the stitches so there is virtually no gap between them. Sew around the design so the left swing of the needle sews into the appliqué and the right swing of the needle is in the base fabric. At outward curves, stop with the needle down in the base fabric, raise the presser foot, swivel the fabric slightly and continue. For inner curves, stop with the needle in the appliqué fabric, raise the presser foot, pivot and then continue.

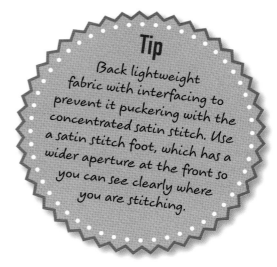

Tip

Back lightweight fabric with interfacing to prevent it puckering with the concentrated satin stitch. Use a satin stitch foot, which has a wider aperture at the front so you can see clearly where you are stitching.

Further appliqué inspiration

1. The centre of this pillow has been stitched with mola appliqué – this is when a design is stitched into several layers of fabric, and then the layers are cut away to reveal the under fabrics – different parts of the design will have different numbers of layers cut away, revealing the different fabrics beneath.

2. Use free-motion stitching to hold an appliqué in place, sewing with a straight stitch around the design several times for a 'naive' look. Add stitch around features of the design also to enhance the motif, like the tail of this elephant.

3. When appliquéing letters and numbers, draw them back to front on the paper backing of the fusible web, so that when turned over and fused in place, they are the right way round.

4. To create free-motion flowerheads, cut fabric circles with pinking shears and then free-motion in a spiral from the centre to the outside edge. Finish the flowers by adding satin stitched stems and leaves.

5. This blue flower is created using reverse appliqué. The appliqué fabric is attached to the underside of the base fabric, and the design stitched around. Then the top layer is cut away to reveal the appliqué. You could then satin stitch or straight stitch around the edge again.

6. This beach hut has been stitched in place with a few different stitches: machine blanket stitch has been used around the outer edge, with straight stitch used around the doors and to define the roof edge. It has been finished with hand sewn French knots for the door handles.

1

2

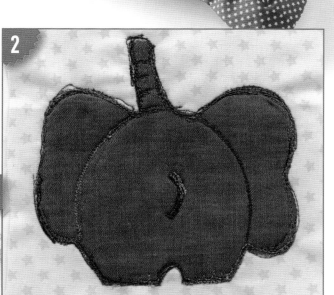

6

3

5

4

Projects

Armed with a collection of lovely fat quarters and some key techniques, you are now ready to dip into your stash and sew. In this selection of fifteen projects there is something for everyone, from simple drawstring bags and fabulous flowers to an appliquéd and quilted playmat for babies, a tucked and stitched pillow cover and a retro apron. The projects are all easy to sew, using simple shapes and minimal piecing so that the fabrics can really stand out. Enjoy making these for yourself or as gifts for friends and family. And remember, never throw remnants away – you can always use even small strips for crazy patchwork or tiny pieces as little appliqué shapes.

Fabulous flowers

Double Suffolk puff: 6cm (2¼in) diameter
Three-petal flower: 7cm (2¾in) diameter
Rosette: 10cm (4in) diameter

Make this trio of flowers to adorn shoes, hairbands, bags or pillows, or to use as corsages. Just two fat quarters will make a number of different flowers.

Variations

- Create an additional puff from a circle of fabric with a 16cm (6¼in) diameter then layer the three puffs together to create a larger flower.

- Make single puffs of different sizes, then use these as a decorative feature on items such as pillows or bags.

- Use a running stitch to sew two circles – each with a diameter of 15cm (6in) – right sides together, leaving a turning gap of about 5cm (2in). Clip the seam allowances and turn through. Press so that the seam is on the edge. Stitch the turning gap closed. Gather all the way around as in step 1 above, then pull up the gathers slightly, leaving a large hole in the centre. Finish the centre with embellishments such as buttons and beads.

- Turn the smaller puff over so that the gathering is on the underside before finishing with one or more buttons, as before.

How to make the flowers

Double Suffolk puff flower

1 Cut two circles of fabric – one with a 12cm (4¾in) diameter, and one with an 8cm (3¼in) diameter. To make life easy for yourself, you could use a CD or DVD and a coffee cup as templates.

2 Thread your needle, pulling the thread through to double it and knot the ends to create a doubled length. Stitch around the edge of your first circle, about 5mm (¼in) from the edge, working all the way round; use a gathering stitch – a long running stitch of about 1cm (½in).

3 Gather up the circle as tightly as possible, with the right side of the fabric on the outside, flattening out the puffiness. Stitch on the spot in the centre to anchor the thread and keep the gathers in place. Repeat with the other circle of fabric.

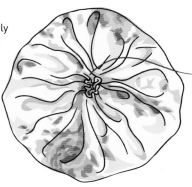

4 Lay the smaller puff on top of the larger one, with the gathered edges facing upwards on each. Stitch the two puffs together through the centres.

5 Finish by stitching a button in the centre of the top puff, taking the threads right through to the back of the lower puff each time to anchor them firmly together.

Three-petal flower

1 Cut three 8cm (3¼in) squares from one of the fat quarters. Fold the squares of fabric in half diagonally with the right sides facing out. Press.

2 Thread the needle with a length of strong or doubled thread and gather stitch along the two short open sides of the triangle, catching the raw edges together. Pull up the stitching to gather the petal into a cup shape, and anchor the thread to secure the gathers. Do not cut the thread.

3 Gather the second and third petal in the same way, attaching each to the same long thread tail to bring all three together.

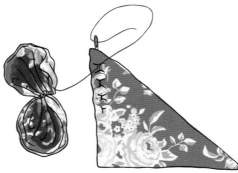

4 To secure the petals together in the centre, stitch through the folds and across the centre several times.

5 Add the larger button to the centre, stitching through all the layers several times. Top with the smaller button, again stitching through all the layers several times.

6 Cover the centre of the underside with a small circle of felt to neaten, and stitch it in place.

Variations

● Make a five-petal flower.

● Cut contrast fabrics to make a layered flower with five petals for the underneath and three petals on top.

● Stitch a brooch back to the circle of felt.

Rosette flower

1 Cut a strip of fabric 8 x 40cm (3 x 15¾in) in one fabric and a smaller strip of 5 x 30cm (2 x 11¾in) from a coordinating fabric. Fold the longer fabric strip right sides together, matching the short ends. Stitch across the short ends to form a ring of fabric. Fold this in half, wrong sides together, to create a slim ring of fabric and press.

2 Thread your needle with a strong or doubled length of thread and knot the end. Sew a running gathering stitch along the raw edges of your ring of fabric. Pull up the stitching to gather the strip into a circle.

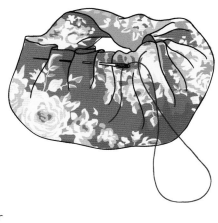

3 Stitch the gathered raw edges together, keeping them tightly connected; stitch across and across again to hold the inner edges securely in place.

4 Repeat steps 1–3 for the smaller strip of fabric. Place the smaller gathered circle on top of the larger one and stitch them together through the middle.

5 Cover a self-cover button with a circle of scrap fabric (see left) and then stitch it to the centre of the flower through both circles to cover the raw edges in the centre neatly.

6 Cover the centre of the underside with a small circle of felt to neaten, and stitch it in place.

Drawstring bags

Lingerie bag: 28 x 25cm (11 x 9¾in)

Shoe bag: 33 x 31cm (13 x 12¼in)

Make some simple bags to hold items such as delicate lingerie or precious shoes. They are very easy to make and can be appliquéd to personalise them.

YOU WILL NEED...

- Two fat quarters
- Fabric remnants for appliqué
- Double-sided fusible web
- 20cm (7¾in) of tearaway stabiliser
- about 1m (1yd) of wide contrasting cord or thin ribbon per bag
- Large safety pin

How to make the shoe bag

1 Cut front and back bag panels 40 x 28cm (15¾ x 11in) and then, using the surplus fabric from the lingerie bag, cut four strips 40 x 4cm (15¾ x 1½in).

2 Fuse the shoe appliqué shapes onto the front of one of the main panels, as for the lingerie bag: back the area with stabiliser then free-motion stitch around the shapes' edges three to four times.

3 Stitch a contrast strip to each long side of the front panel: place the fabrics right sides together and sew taking a 5mm (¼in) seam allowance. Repeat for the back panel using the other two strips.

4 Make up the bag following steps 3–7 for the lingerie bag.

How to make the lingerie bag

1 Cut two pieces of fabric, 34 x 28cm (13¼ x 11in), to form the front and back of the bag. Set the rest aside for the shoe bag. Position the appliqué shapes on the right side of one of the bag panels, approximately 10cm (4in) up from the short bottom edge. When you are happy with their position, peel away the paper backing and fuse them in place with a hot iron – protect your work with a press cloth while you do so. Back the area with tearaway stabiliser.

2 Stitch around the edges of the appliqué shapes using free-motion stitching, roughly three to four times. Draw straps for the bra in a disappearing pen and then free-motion stitch these too. Tear away any excess stabiliser from the back of the fabric.

3 On the wrong side of the bag front, mark the casing position: measure down the side edges by 6cm (2¼in) and mark on either side. Mark down a further 2cm (¾in). Place the bag front and back right sides together and, taking a 1cm (½in) seam allowance, stitch the side seams from the top edge to the first mark. Backstitch to secure the stitching. Start stitching again at the second mark, leaving the casing section unstitched. Again, backstitch at the start to secure the stitching, then continue to the bottom of the bag. At the bottom, pivot with the needle down and stitch bottom edge. Pivot again at the second corner then stitch the second side edge as the first, leaving the casing section unstitched.

4 Neaten and strengthen the raw edges by zigzag stitching in the seam allowance and then trimming the seams close to the stitching.

5 Still with the bag wrong side out, create a gusseted bottom by refolding the bag so that the side seams sit on top of the bottom seam to create triangles at the bottom side edges. Stitch across the triangle about 3cm (1¼in) from the tip (see illustration). Trim the excess triangles off and neaten the raw edges with zigzag stitch again. Turn the bag the right way out; press.

6 To make the casing, turn under the top edge by 5cm (2in), tucking the raw edge under again by 1cm (½in) and press. Stitch all the way round, close to the turned-under fold, which should be just below the open seam section at the side edges. Stitch a parallel row of stitches 2cm (¾in) above the first row to create your channel.

7 Cut your piece of ribbon or cord into two equal lengths. Using a safety pin, feed one end of the ribbon through the casing all the way around and out the same side (see illustration). Knot the ends together. Feed the second piece of ribbon from the other side edge, again all the way around, and then knot the ends together.

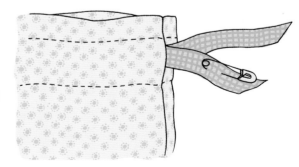

Reversible bag

16 x 23cm (6¼ x 9in), excluding handles

Make this pretty and petite handbag as a gift or
to hold essentials on a dressing table.

YOU WILL NEED...

- Two fat quarters
- 40 x 50cm (15¾ x 19¾in) wadding (batting)
- 1m (39in) of 1cm (½in) wide ribbon
- Small bag of toy stuffing
- Magnetic clasp (optional)
- 50cm (19¾in) length of 1cm (½in) wide contrasting ribbon (optional)

How to make the bag

1 Cut two rectangles of 25 x 19cm (10 x 7½in) from each of the fat quarters – two for the outside of the bag, two for the reversible lining. Also cut two rectangles of the same size from the wadding (batting).

2 Cut two strips of 6 x 25cm (2⅜ x 10in) for the handles.

3 Cut and pin two lengths of ribbon to the piece of fabric you will use for the front of the bag: place one length along the long bottom edge of the bag, 6cm (2⅜in) up from the bottom, and the other length up the right-hand side of the bag, 6cm (2⅜in) in from the right-hand edge. Trim the ribbon so that its ends align with the fabric edges. Repeat for the piece of fabric that will form the back of the bag.

4 Position the wadding (batting) rectangles behind the main bag pieces, and then with thread colour to match the ribbon, stitch in place along both long edges of each piece of ribbon, anchoring the wadding (batting) in place as you do so.

5 With right sides together, sew the main bag pieces together along the sides and the bottom edge, taking a 5mm (¼in) seam allowance. Press the seams open.

6 Create a bag base by refolding a side seam to sit on top of the bottom seam, creating a triangular corner. Sew across the triangle about 5cm (2in) from the tip. Cut off the triangle and neaten the seam. Repeat for the other corner. Set aside.

7 To create the handles, fold the strips right sides together and stitch across one short end and up the long edge. Turn through and stuff firmly with toy stuffing, pushing in a little at a time and tamping it down. Leave each end unstuffed by about 1cm (½in).

8 Pin and stitch the ends of one handle to the top edge of the bag. Position the pieces right sides together, with the handle hanging down towards the bag and the ends approximately 6cm (2³⁄₈in) in from each side seam. Stitch in place within the seam allowance. Repeat for the bag back with the other handle.

9 Pin the lining pieces right sides together and stitch along the side and bottom edges, with a 5mm (¼in) seam allowance, leaving a 15cm (6in) turning gap in the bottom edge. Create the bag base as in step 6.

10 Add the magnetic clasp pieces to the lining bag: find the centre of the top edge of the bag and mark 3cm (1¼in) down. Using the washer of the clasp as a guide, mark the fabric at the 3cm (1¼in) position. Snip into the fabric at these marks and push the clasp prongs though from the right side of lining. Add a small square of wadding (batting) behind, again snipping holes, and push the prongs through. Place the washer on top and then fold the prongs back to anchor the clasp. Repeat for the other half of the clasp on the other side of the lining.

11 With the main bag right side out, slip it inside the lining bag, which is wrong side out – the right sides of the bag and the lining should be facing, and the handles should be sandwiched between the layers. Stitch around the top of bag 1cm (½in) from the top edge. Turn the bag through the opening in the bottom of the lining. Slip stitch the opening closed and push the lining inside the bag. Press the top edge, rolling the lining to the inside so that the seam is on the edge. Top-stitch around the bag top to hold the lining firmly in place.

12 Using the second contrast ribbon, make up two little bows and stitch to either side of the bag, just under the handles.

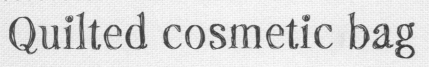

Quilted cosmetic bag

10 x 14 x 7cm (4 x 5½ x 2¾in)

Make this boxy make-up bag with quilted sides and a zip fastening – it's easier than it looks.

YOU WILL NEED...

- Two fat quarters: one for outer bag, one for lining
- 52 x 42cm (20½ x 16½in) wadding (batting)
- 18cm (7in) zip
- Zip foot, walking foot and quilting guide (optional)

Preparation

From the fat quarter cut:

- One piece for the bottom of the bag, 21 x 26cm (8¼ x 10¼in)

- Two pieces for the top of the bag, 11.5 x 26cm (4½ x 10¼in)

- Cut lining pieces as above either from the same fabric or a contrast fabric

- Cut wadding (batting) as above

How to make the bag

1 Take the two smaller bag pieces and pin them right sides together. Position the zip along the centre of one long side, about 1cm (½in) in from the edge, and mark the fabric at the top of the zip (where the zip pull is) and at the bottom of the zip where the teeth finish. Set the zip aside for the moment. (See page 28 for more information.)

2 You will now need to sew along the long edge where your zip will be. Sew the seam with a 1cm (½in) seam allowance from the fabric edge to the first mark, backstitching when you reach it to lock your stitching. Then machine baste (tack) the zip opening by increasing your stitch length to maximum: start stitching 5cm (2in) along from the first mark (without backstitching) until the second zip mark is reached. Change your stitch length back to regular 2.5 and continue the seam to the end. Press the seam allowance open.

3 Place the zip face down on top of the pressed-open seam, with the teeth running along the seam line and the top of the zip in line with the 5cm (2in) gap left unstitched. Pin and baste (tack) in position.

4 Turn the fabric over to the right side. With a zip foot on your machine, stitch the zip in place through all thicknesses, starting at the base of the zip at the seam. Make three or four stitches across the bottom, then, with the needle down, pivot the fabric to stitch up the side. When close to the zip pull, again stop with the needle down, raise the presser foot and push the zip pull below the stitching. Continue to the end. Repeat for the other side of the zip.

5 Pin the wadding (batting) pieces to the reverse of your zipped piece, butting the wadding (batting) up against the zip tape. Quilt in place using a grid pattern: start with parallel lines stitched across the width, then sew vertically from the zip out to the edge, spacing the lines about 2.5cm (1in) apart.

6 Add wadding (batting) to the other main piece in the same way. Quilt in a grid with horizontal and vertical lines as before, keeping the same 2.5cm (1in) spacing between your lines of stitching. Trim the edges to square up if necessary.

Tip

Use a walking foot with a quilting guide to help stitch perfectly parallel rows every time.

7 To make the bag corners, measure and mark up and in 5cm (2in) on each corner on both the quilted panels. Cut away the marked squares as shown.

8 Unpick the basting (tacking) stitches and open the zip. Place your two quilted pieces on top of each other, with right sides together. Sew front to back along the top, bottom and sides, leaving the cut-out square sections unsewn.

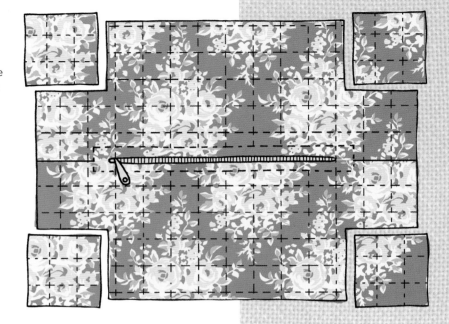

9 Bring the cut-out square edges together to form a seam at each of the corners and stitch together; press.

10 You will now need to create your lining. Pin your two smaller pieces together, right sides facing. As in step 2 you will need to sew them together at either end of this long edge, leaving a gap in the middle long enough to accommodate the zip. Press the seams and zip opening open. Place this seamed piece of fabric on top of your larger piece of lining fabric, right sides facing. Mark and cut a 5cm (2in) square away at each of the corners. As in step 8, sew along the outside edges, leaving the cut-out square sections unsewn. Sew up the corners as in step 9.

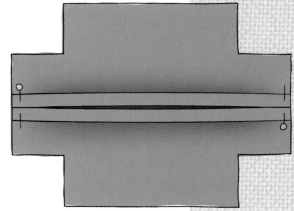

11 Turn the lining right side out and slip the main bag inside, so that the wrong sides are facing each other. Slip stitch the lining to the bag around the zip tape. Turn the bag the right way out.

Door stop

16 x 16 x 16cm (6¼ x 6¼ x 6¼in), excluding handle

Make a pretty door stop to keep the door from slamming.
Pretty trims and buttons add decoration.

YOU WILL NEED...

- Two fat quarters
- Six buttons (five of one colour for the petals, one for the flower centre)
- 20cm (7¾in) lengths of four to six different trims or lace
- 50cm (19¾in) of pelmet interfacing or heavy-weight interfacing
- 10 x 20cm (4 x 7¾in) strip of wadding (batting)
- Toy stuffing
- Bag of lentils or rice

Preparation

● Cut three 18cm (7in) squares of fabric from each of the fat quarters

● Cut a handle strip, 21 x 11cm (8¼ x 4¼in), from one of the fat quarters

● Cut six squares of 18cm (7in) from the interfacing

How to make the door stop

1 Take your first fabric square and with interfacing behind it, machine stitch a flower stem using satin stitch (zigzag stitch with a stitch length of 0.4 and a width of 3). Add a leaf in straight stitch. Then hand or machine stitch buttons in a flower shape at the top of the stem, with a contrast button in the centre.

2 Take your second fabric square and with interfacing behind it, machine stitch two lengths of ribbon and a length of lace across the width. Stitch close to the edge of each piece by moving the needle to the far right or left. Stitch both side edges of the ribbon in the same direction to prevent the ribbon twisting. Stitch the lace along one long edge only.

3 Taking your third fabric square, place interfacing behind it and stitch a length of ribbon across it as in step 2. Add a further length of ribbon at right angles to the first.

4 With interfacing behind it, add a decorative trim to the fourth square. When applying a bobble trim, use a zip foot and straight stitch to stitch close to the bobbles if necessary. The four squares decorated in steps 1–4 will make up the sides of the cube doorstop.

5 Place two alternating coloured squares right sides together and sew down one side edge taking a 5mm (¼in) seam allowance. Open out. Repeat for the other two decorated squares. Then with right sides facing again, stitch the two panels together to join the four sides of the cube. Set aside.

6 To create your handle, turn one long edge of the handle strip to the wrong side by 5mm (¼in) and press. Lay your wadding (batting) strip in the centre of the wrong side, then fold the raw fabric edge to the centre. Fold the wadding (batting) in the process. Lap the neatened edge over the centred raw edge. Machine stitch down the centre through all layers. Stitch again either side of the centre row of stitching.

7 Pin and stitch the handle to two opposite sides of the cube, so that the raw edges are aligned and the handle is centred along the top edge of the cube sides – please note that the handle will hang down inside the cube.

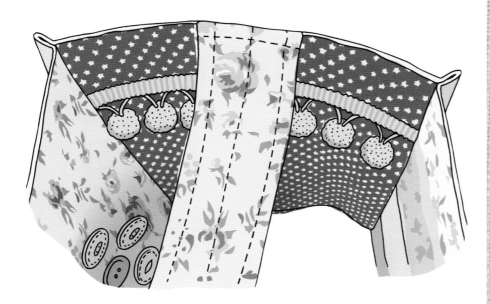

8 Interface the remaining two squares and then pin the top panel of the cube in place, right side facing in, pinning around the edges holding the top to the sides. Machine stitch, starting in the middle of one edge, stitch to within 5mm (¼in) of the corner, backstitch. Take out of the sewing machine. Refold so you can stitch the second edge, starting 5mm (¼in) from the edge so that the stitching from the previous side meets the start of the new side. Continue around the top.

9 Pin the bottom panel to the cube, right sides together. Start sewing about 3cm (1¼in) from one corner, stitch to within 5mm (¼in) of the corner, as in step 8, then refold and continue to stitch around the square. Stop stitching halfway along the third side, leaving a turning gap of approximately one-and-a-half sides. Clip away any excess fabric at the corners at an angle and then turn the cube through.

10 Pack with toy stuffing until three-quarters full, ensuring that you push the stuffing right into the corners. Add a bag of rice or lentils and then slip stitch the opening closed. Turn up the right way so the handle is at the top and the rice bag falls to the bottom.

Party clutch

15.5 x 21cm (6 x 8¼in)

Create a textured surface on a pretty fabric using the
bubble technique and then transform it into a clutch bag.

Bubble technique

Using two layers of fusible web and one of soluble stabiliser, plus lots of steam, you can create a shirring effect on fabric. The fabric shrinks to about two-thirds of its original size, so for this bag front, a fabric piece of 31 x 19cm (12¼ x 7½in) shrinks to approximately 23 x 14cm (9 x 5½in).

1 Cut a 31 x 19cm (12¼ x 7½in) piece from the main fabric.

2 Fuse two layers of fusible web to the back of the fabric piece: fuse one, remove the paper backing and fuse the second one. Remove the paper backing of the second fusible web layer and fuse on a layer of soluble stabiliser.

3 Stitch parallel rows of straight stitching, approximately 1cm (½in) apart, across the width of the fabric piece. Once complete, working on the ironing mat, hover a steam iron above the wrong side of the fabric and watch it shrink as the steam heats and dissolves some of the stabiliser. Leave to cool for one hour.

4 Hand wash the piece to remove the rest of the stabiliser. The fabric will remain crisper or harder than the original even after one or two washes. To get it back to a softer handle, wash in a machine.

How to make the clutch

1 Sew the bag flap to the main bag piece – along a long edge of the bag flap and a short edge of the main bag piece – right sides together, taking a 1cm (½in) seam. Press the seam.

2 Layer all the fabrics as follows: lining right side down, pelmet interfacing, wadding (batting) and then the main fabric right side up. Pin the layers together and then quilt the main section starting with a line diagonally from top left to bottom right. Set the stitch length to 3 and continue to stitch parallel rows of straight stitching, about 4cm (1½in) apart, either side of the first, using a quilting guide – if available – to ensure perfectly parallel rows (see page 24).

3 Draw another line diagonally from top right to bottom left and stitch as before. Stitch around the outside edge of the textured flap. Trim all the layers evenly all the way around.

4 Make a loop from the ribbon. Alternatively, make a rouleau loop as I did (see page 31). Position it on the right side of the front of the bag flap, in the centre of the top edge, with the loop towards the bag and the ends aligned with the edge of the bag flap. Stitch in place.

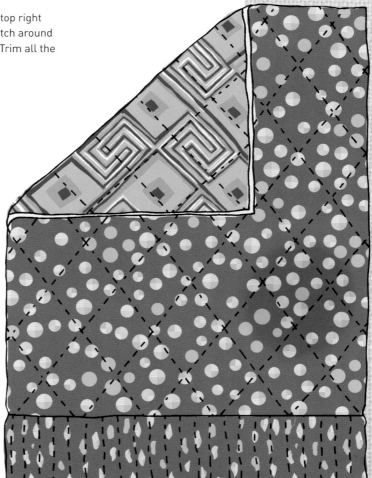

Tip
Layering the fabrics and quilting through them all at the same time neatly attaches the lining to the bag quickly and easily.

5 To bind your top edge, fold under one long edge of your binding by 5mm (¼in) and press. Pin and stitch the unfolded long edge of the binding to the bag's top edge, right sides together, sandwiching the ribbon loop ends.

6 Fold the binding over to the lining side, encasing the raw edges. Pin from the right side, folding the loop back up so that it is facing away from the bag. Stitch the binding in place on the very edge, from the right side, catching the back of the binding as you go. Repeat for the bottom edge of the bag.

7 Fold the bag bottom up by approximately 13cm (5in) to form the bag shape. Stitch the side seams with a 5mm (¼in) seam on the outside of the bag.

8 If necessary, join pieces of binding fabric together to make strips that are long enough to bind each side edge: make these strips about 1cm (½in) longer than each edge, so that the ends can be turned under. To add binding to each side edge, fold under one long edge and each short end of your piece of binding by 5mm (¼in) and press. Pin the unfolded long edge of the binding to the opened bag, with right sides together and the raw edges aligned. Sew it in place, as shown. Fold the binding to the other side, encasing the raw edge, and stitch close to the edge of the binding as in step 7 above.

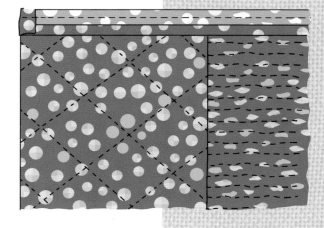

9 Hand sew the button to the bag front.

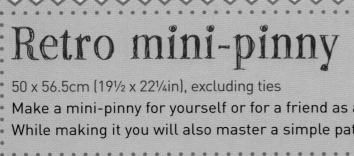

Retro mini-pinny

50 x 56.5cm (19½ x 22¼in), excluding ties

Make a mini-pinny for yourself or for a friend as a gift at Christmas.
While making it you will also master a simple patch pocket and ruffles.

How to make the mini-pinny

1 Fold the main apron fabric piece in half lengthways and place in front of you on a flat surface, with the short edges at the top and bottom. Mark 45cm (17¾in) up from the bottom edge. Draw across the folded fabric at this mark and cut away the excess. Place a dinner plate or other round object on the bottom open corner and draw a curved hemline around it. Cut away the excess.

2 Create a heart pocket template from a piece of card, approximately 15cm (6in) wide and 15cm (6in) tall. Fold your remnant fabric in half and pin the heart template on the fabric. Draw round it then cut out to create two heart shapes.

3 Place the two heart shapes right sides together, then sew around the edge leaving a 4cm (1½in) turning gap in one side. Clip into the seam allowance at the curves then turn through. Press with the seams on the edges, tucking the turning gap seam allowances to the inside.

4 Position the heart-shaped pocket on the apron front, 21cm (8¼in) down from the top edge and 8cm (3¼in) in from the right side edge. Pin and stitch around the sides, stitching very close to the pocket edge, and leaving the curved top edge of the heart open.

5 From contrast fabric, cut four strips 12cm (4¾in) wide across the width of the fat quarter. Join the short ends together to create one long strip. Press the joins open, then fold the strip in half, wrong sides together, and press.

6 Find the central point in the length of the folded strip and mark with a pin. Find the middle of the apron's bottom edge and mark with a pin. Align these two centre points and pin the folded strip to the edge of the apron, right sides together, with the raw edges matching. Match up and pin each end in place at the top of the apron, again with right sides facing and raw edges aligned – this will create some slack in your folded strip. Take small pleats in the strip, pinning them to the apron as you go until all the fullness is taken up (here I made thirty-four pleats, each about 3cm (1¼in) wide). Once evenly pleated and pinned securely around the apron edge, stitch in place with a straight stitch, taking a 5mm (¼in) seam allowance.

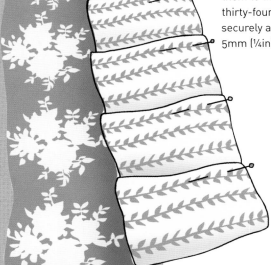

7 Open out the pleated edging and press so that the seam allowances are pressed towards the apron. Using a zigzag stitch with the length set at 2.5 and the width set at 2, zigzag stitch from the right side all around the apron, close to the pleated edge, catching the seam allowances in place as you go.

8 You will next need to create an inverted pleat at the top of the apron. Find the centre of the top edge, then measure and mark 6cm (2¼in) either side. Take a fold at the 6cm (2¼in) marks and bring the folds to the centre. Pin and stitch in place close to the top edge, as shown in the illustration, right.

9 Gather the remaining top edge either side of the pleat by stitching 5mm (¼in) from edge, using the longest stitch length. Pull up the bobbin thread to evenly gather the fabric.

10 To create the bias-binding waistband, find the centre of the bias binding and the centre of the apron's top edge and mark each with a pin. Fold the binding in half lengthways and wrap over the top of the apron, matching the centre pin marks. Pin through all the layers from side edge to side edge and then pin the binding together for the ties, tucking the raw ends inside.

11 Select a decorative stitch or simple zigzag stitch and matching thread and stitch the bias binding to the apron top from side to side, catching both edges of the bias binding as you go. Continue stitching along to each tie end. Press the apron again.

Diamond-star mat

51 x 57cm (20 x 22½in)

Make a pretty table centrepiece in fabrics to match your home décor. Not only does it look lovely, it will protect the surface of your table.

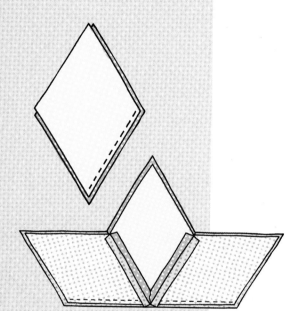

How to make the mat

1 Fold your first fat quarter in half widthways with the right sides together. Using the triangle template on page 94, mark out the first half diamond, with one straight edge of the triangle on the fold of fabric. Cut out along the two open side edges – when you open out the triangle of fabric you will have a diamond shape. Repeat to create two more diamonds from the same fabric.

2 Repeat step 1 with the second fabric to create three more diamonds.

3 Sew two contrasting diamonds together along one edge, right sides facing, leaving a 5mm (¼in) seam allowance at either end of your stitching, and between your stitching and the fabric edge. Open out your diamonds. In the same way, attach a third diamond to this piece, to create a shape with a straight lower edge; position it so that the contrast fabric is in the middle of two the same.

4 Repeat for the remaining three diamonds.

5 Join the two pieces, right sides together, along their straight edges as shown left – if necessary cutting the edges into a neat straight line with a rotary cutter. Press the seams to the darkest fabric side.

6 Lay the wadding (batting) on a flat surface, top with remaining fabric, right side up and then with the star, right side down. Pin through all the layers around the star edges. Stitch around the shape, taking a 5mm (¼in) seam allowance, leaving a turning gap in one side.

7 Trim the seam allowances, clipping into the angles close to the stitching and snipping the points across close to the stitching. Turn through, pushing out the points. Slip stitch the opening closed.

8 Finish with some quilting in metallic thread. Attach a metallic needle and thread then, working slowly, stitch 5mm (¼in) around the edges and then from the centre approximately 18cm (7¼in) into each point. Now stitch between the lines just made and the edges of the diamond, making the lines about 6cm (2½in) long. You do not have to put metallic thread in the bobbin unless you want to – you can use thread to match the fabric.

Al fresco placemat

34cm (13¼in) diameter

Make placemats with cutlery catchers for outdoor dining. Using strips
that are sewn at angles gives the circular mats a crazy-patch appeal.

Preparation for each placemat

- Cut four strips of 7 x 35cm (2¾ x 13½in) from one fat quarter and five strips of 7 x 35cm (2¾ x 13½in) from the other

- Cut two small strips of 12 x 7cm (4¾ x 2¾in) for the cutlery catchers

How to make the mat

1 Lay two contrasting strips right sides together. Keeping the top-left edges together, swing the bottom of the upper layer to the right, so that the bottom-left edge of the upper layer is 1cm (³/₈in) from the right-hand edge of the lower layer. Pin the two pieces together then stitch with a 5mm (¼in) seam. Cut off the excess underlayer.

2 Flip the top layer over and add another strip, this time, with top-right edges together and the bottom-right edge moved diagonally across to the left. Again stitch with a 5mm (¼in) seam. Flip and continue adding contrasting strips at angles until all nine are used. Press all the seams.

3 On the reverse of the fabric, draw around the bowl or plate with a disappearing or fadeaway marking pen. Cut out 1cm (½in) outside the marked line; the marked line will be your stitching line.

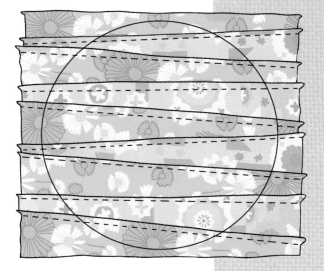

4 Cut the same size circles from backing fabric and wadding (batting). Use two layers of insulated wadding (batting) to protect your surfaces from hot plates.

5 Place the wadding (batting) on a flat surface, then the backing fabric right side up, followed by the front panel right side down. Pin around the edges.

6 Increase your stitch length to 3.5 and stitch through all the layers around your marked circular line, leaving a turning gap of approximately 12cm (4¾in). Trim the seams and snip into the seam allowance at an angle – this will help to produce a smooth curved outline when the mat is turned through. Turn through. Press so that the seam is on the edge, tucking the raw edges of the turning gap inside. Slip stitch the gap closed.

Tip
Use two layers of insulated wadding (batting), which will help to protect your surfaces from heat.

7 Fold one of the small strips right sides together, so that it measures 12 x 3.5cm (4¾ x 1³/₈in), and stitch along the two short ends, taking a 5mm (¼in) seam allowance. Clip away the excess fabric at the corners and turn the piece through. Press.

8 Cut a length of bias binding 14cm (5½in) long. Tuck the short ends under and press. Wrap the bias binding around the long raw edge of the strip created in step 7. Pin and stitch the binding in place, close to the edge. Repeat steps 7 and 8 with the other small strip. These strips will hold your cutlery in place.

9 Lay a knife, fork and spoon to the right-hand side of the mat to determine the position of the strips. Start with the lower strip: place it over the cutlery, about 2.5cm (1in) from the bottom. Pin at the side edges and between each item of cutlery to create three channels. Repeat with the other strip at the top of the cutlery handles. Remove the cutlery and stitch down the pinned lines.

10 Finish by stitching around the outside edge of the mat, 1cm (½in) from the edge and using a 3.5 stitch length.

Tucked and stitched pillow

35.5 x 35.5cm (14 x 14in), without pillow pad

Use decorative stitching and creative tucks to make a beautiful pillow cover with textured detail.

Preparation

- Cut the tuck fabric to 30 x 40cm (11¾ x 15¾in)

Cut the remaining fat quarters as follows:

- One piece, 25 x 40cm (9¾ x 15¾in), for the decorative stitched panel

- Two pieces for the back, each 23 x 40cm (9 x 15¾in)

- Interface the back of the panel for decorative stitching

How to make the pillow

1 Starting with the tuck fabric, fold in half lengthways to find the centre and press to mark. Unfold then, using a disappearing marking pen, draw a line from top to bottom 4cm (1½in) away from the crease. Continue to do this either side of the crease leaving the last 4cm (1½in) or so either side unmarked.

2 To make the tucks, fold the fabric at the centre crease with the wrong sides together and place under your presser foot with the fold lined up with the right edge of the presser foot. Move the needle position to the right so that you sew approximately 5mm (¼in) from the folded edge. Sew from top to bottom. Unfold the fabric, then make the next tuck by folding the fabric again along the nearest marked line to the right; stitch the second tuck in the same way. Continue this way to stitch all the tucks on the right-hand side.

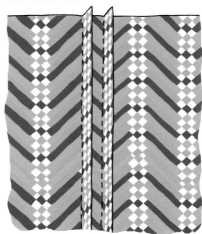

3 Turn the work up the other way before you stitch the tucks on the left hand side – this will mean that they are all folded in the same direction. Once you have sewn all your tucks, press them in the same direction.

4 Mark horizontally across the tucks every 8cm (3¼in); start in the centre, working out to each side. Stitch along the centre line, across all the tucks, so that they are all stitched down in the same direction. Sew along all your marked horizontal lines, stitching the tucks down.

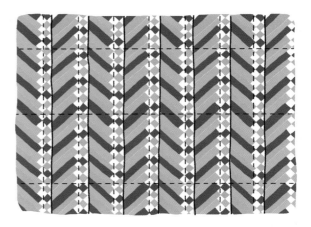

Tip

Use a ¼in (0.5cm) presser foot to ensure an accurate distance from the fold of the fabric to the stitch line.

Tip

Rather than marking all the stitching lines in step 4, stitch down the centre line then use a quilter's guide positioned so it is 8cm (3¼in) from the needle. Use the guide to stitch perfectly parallel rows (see Quilting, page 24).

5 Mark further horizontal lines between the stitched lines created in step 4: mark centrally between each set of lines, 4cm (1½in) from each. Turn the work round so that you will be sewing across the fabric in the other direction and as you sew, pull each of the tucks towards you.

6 Press along each line of stitching very carefully with the tip of an iron.

7 It's now time to create your decorative stitched panel; you will sew the lines of stitching along the length of the piece. Mark the centre of the panel with a disappearing pen from top to bottom and then, using a decorative stitch and contrast thread colour in the top of your machine, sew the first line of stitching. Either mark equidistant lines from the first and sew either side, using a different stitch, or use the quilter's guide along the first line of stitching to create the second and subsequent lines in parallel.

8 Continue to sew decorative stitches along the panel length. To make sure that the two halves are mirror images of each other, select stitches that have equally balanced right and left swings, or that work equally if stitched top to bottom on the right, and bottom to top on the left. Leave at least 4cm (1½in) either side of the panel undecorated.

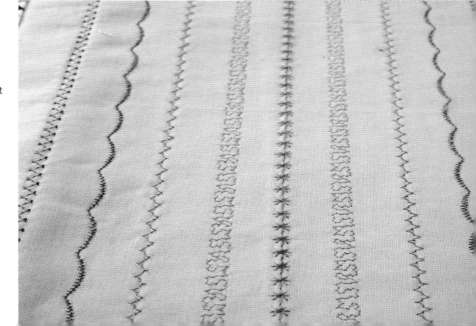

9 With right sides together, sew the tucked panel to the decorated panel along one long edge. Press and trim to a 40cm (15¾in) square if needed.

10 With right sides together, pin the two back panels together. Place the zip centrally on the seam on one long edge, and mark the beginning and end of the zip teeth. Remove the zip. Taking a 2cm (¾in) seam allowance, machine stitch from the fabric edge to the first mark using a normal stitch length, then backstitch to secure the stiches. Leave a gap of 5cm (2in), then increase the stitch to the longest possible length and machine baste (tack) until you reach the second mark. Reduce the stitch length to normal again to continue the seam, remembering to backstitch at the start and finish to fix the stitching. Press the seam allowance open. (See also pages 28–29.)

11 Position the zip face down over the pressed-open seam allowance, with the zip pull over the 5cm (2in) gap in the stitching, and pin or hand baste (tack) in position – if pinning, do so from the right side of the fabric.

12 Attach a zip foot and, starting at the bottom end, in the centre at the seam, machine stitch at right angles to the seam along the bottom of the zip, then pivot and stitch up the side of the zip approximately 5mm (¼in) from the seam. As you get close to the zip pull, with the needle down, raise the presser foot and work the zip pull down below the needle. Continue to sew to the end. Repeat for other side of the zip, again starting at the base of the zip. Use a quick unpick to undo the basting (tacking) stitches and free your zip.

13 Open the zip. Place the front and back sides of the pillow cover right sides together. Stitch around the edge of the cover, taking a 1cm (½in) seam allowance. Neaten the raw edges with an overlock stitch or zigzag stitch. Trim the seam allowances and press. Turn the pillow cover through and press again. Insert the pillow pad.

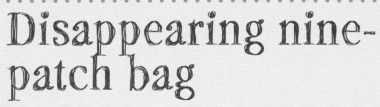

Disappearing nine-patch bag

33 x 37cm (13 x 14½in), excluding handles

This design looks a lot of hard work, but really it is deceptively simple, and makes a stylish, practical bag.

Preparation

● From each of the three coordinating fabrics, cut six squares of 15cm (6in): eighteen squares in total

● From what is left of one of the fabrics cut two handles, 7 x 32cm (2¾ x 12½in)

How to make the bag

1 Taking a 5mm (¼in) seam allowance, sew three squares together, one of each fabric, to make a strip of three different fabrics. Repeat this with six more squares so that you have three strips of three: use a different fabric in the centre of the strip each time.

2 Sew two strips together along one long edge, matching up the cross seams carefully. To keep the cross seams matching perfectly, pin the strips together at the seams first, then match the side edges. Attach the third strip in the same way to create a nine-patch square.

3 Iron the panel, pressing the seams flat. You will now need to quarter your nine-patch square: fold it in half and press it to mark the centre point, unfold then fold in half the other way and press; unfold. Working on a flat surface, cut along the creases to cut the panel into four quarters.

4 Turn the top-right and the bottom-left quarter around by one turn clockwise. Pin the two right-hand pieces together again and stitch with a 5mm (¼in) seam. Repeat for the two left-hand pieces and then join the left to right strips, again taking care to match seams where they meet. You now have a disappearing nine-patch panel. Repeat for the other nine squares to make the bag back.

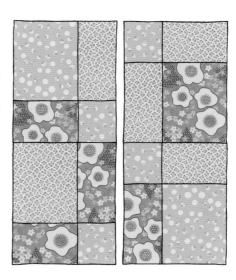

5 At the bottom corners of both the front and back pieces, mark 5cm (2in) squares up from bottom and in from the edge. Cut off the squares.

6 Cut wadding (batting) to the same size as each panel and anchor in place to the reverse of the panel by stitching in the ditch – to stitch in the ditch, sew along the seamlines joining the patches together.

7 Place your front and back panels right sides together and stitch along the sides and the bottom edge, leaving the cut-out squares unstitched, and taking a 1cm (½in) seam allowance.

8 Bring the cut-out square edges together to form a seam at each bottom corner – the side seam and bottom seam will be one on top of the other – and stitch together. Finish by zigzag stitching the seam. Turn the bag through to the right side; press.

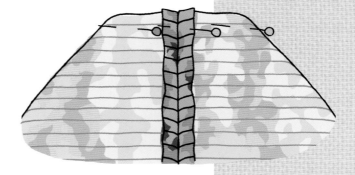

9 To make the handles: press a narrow hem along one side of a strip of handle fabric. Lay it down with the wrong side facing up. Cut a strip of wadding (batting) that is 2.5cm (1in) wide and the length of the handle, and place centrally on top of the handle fabric. Fold the unhemmed long edge into the centre and press. Fold the hemmed edge over to lap over the raw edge. Machine stitch down the centre of the handle to catch the lapped edges and again along either long edge twice to make it strong (so you have four or five lines down the length of the handle).

10 Pin the handle ends to the right side of the bag top, approximately 14cm (5½in) in from each side, with the raw edges aligned and with the handle straps pointing down, as shown. Machine stitch the top edges into place.

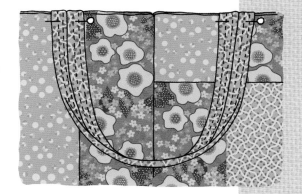

11 To make the lining, cut two pieces of fabric 37cm (14½in) square. Follow step 5 to cut away a square in each of the bottom corners.

12 To add an optional pocket, cut a piece of fabric to 40 x 10cm (16 x 4in). Fold in half with right sides together to create a 20 x 10cm (8 x 4in) rectangle. Stitch around the outside with a 5mm (¼in) seam, leaving a turning gap in one long edge – this will be the bottom edge of your pocket. Clip the seams, cutting away the excess fabric at the corners at an angle. Turn the piece through and press, with the seams on the edge. Stitch across the top edge of the pocket piece, 5mm (¼in) from the edge and press again. Position the pocket on the right side of one lining section, 9cm (3½in) from the top edge. Stitch to the lining along the sides and bottom, catching the turning gap in the stitching, and stitching a scant 2–3mm (⅛in) from the edges of the pocket. If you want to create divisions to hold items such as pens, keys or your phone, sew dividing lines accordingly.

13 Pin and stitch the lining pieces, right sides together, along the sides and bottom edge, leaving the cut-out squares unstitched and leaving a turning gap of at least 18cm (7in) in the bottom edge. Stitch the bottom corners as in step 8.

14 You now need to add your magnetic clasp. Find the centre of the lining top edge and mark it with a pin. Place the magnetic clasp washer about 5cm (2in) down from the top edge and mark the position. Snip into the fabric for the prongs of the clasp. Push the clasp through the fabric from the right side. Cut a small piece of wadding (batting) and push the prongs through this also, on the wrong side of the fabric. Add the washer, bending the prongs over to hold clasp in place. Repeat on the other piece of lining, again working from the right side of the fabric to attach the other half of the clasp. Make sure the two sections line up.

15 To sew the lining in place, insert the bag, right sides out, inside the lining which is wrong sides out, so that the right sides of bag and lining face each other and the handles are sandwiched between them. Make sure the side seams and tops of the bags are aligned then pin them together. Stitch around the top edge, taking a 15mm (⅝in) seam allowance. Trim the seam, press, then turn the bag the right way out through the turning gap left in the bottom edge of the lining. Slip stitch the turning gap closed.

16 Push the lining inside the bag and press. Machine stitch around the top edge to secure the lining in place, 1cm (½in) from the edge.

Draught excluder

8 x 91 x 10.5cm (3¼ x 35¾ x 4¼in)

Use up fabric and trimming scraps to make a draught excluder that's practical as well as eye-catchingly pretty.

YOU WILL NEED...

– Twelve fabric strips, measuring 38 x 10cm (15 x 4in)

– 76cm (30in) of 2cm (¾in) wide ribbon trim

– 76cm (30in) of 2cm (¾in) wide lace trim

– 38cm (15in) of 1cm (½in) wide ribbon

– 350g (12½oz) toy stuffing

How to make the draught excluder

1 Lay out your strips to determine which will go next to each other. Once you are happy with the arrangement, start at one end and, with right sides together, stitch two of the strips together along one long edge taking a narrow 6mm (¼in) seam. Open out.

2 Cut the lace trim into two equal lengths of 38cm (15in). Lay one of the lace trims, right sides together along the edge of the second strip (so that the straight edge of the trim is along the raw edge of the strip). Pin and stitch the third strip to the second, right sides together again, sandwiching the trim in the seam.

3 Stitch the next seven strips in place to create a set of ten joined strips.

4 Add the second lace strip to the right edge of the tenth strip as in step 2 above. Again, sandwich this trim with the next (eleventh) strip and stitch, right sides together. Add the remaining strip to complete the fabric piecing.

5 With the panel flat, right side up, count along to the seam between strips six and seven. Lay the narrow ribbon centred over the seam and sew in place down both long edges of the ribbon.

6 Divide the wide ribbon into two equal lengths and repeat step 5, stitching the ribbon lengths over the seams of panels five and six and seven and eight. Press the ribboned seams again.

7 Fold the whole piece in half lengthways, right sides together, matching the seams of each panel, and press again. At each of the four corners, mark up the edge and in from the edge by 5cm (2in); cut off the four little squares marked.

8 Sew the short ends, leaving the cut-out sections unsewn. Then sew along the long edge, leaving a turning gap of approximately 15cm (6in) in the centre.

9 To make the boxy corners: bring the cut edges of the cut-out corners together. With the seam in the centre, stitch the seam. Repeat for the other three corners. Turn the panel through to the right side and press with the long seam centred in the panel.

10 Stuff with toy stuffing, pushing it right into the boxy ends. Do not over-stuff; if the draught excluder is slightly floppy it will stay snugly against the door more easily. Hand-stitch the opening closed.

Tip

Use the first square cut-off as a template for the other three corners.

Pillow with piping

35.5 x 35.5cm (14 x 14in), without pillow pad

Use a simple patchwork technique and add piping,
for a pillow with 'wow' factor.

Preparation

From the first fat quarter cut:

- A pentagonal centre patch cut from a 15cm 6in square (or cut this from the contrast fabric)
- Pillow back, 30 x 40cm (11¾ x 15¾in)
- Three or four strips varying in width from 4–6cm (1½–2¼in)

From the second fat quarter cut

- Pillow back, 30 x 40cm (11¾ x 15¾in)
- Two long border pieces, 9 x 40cm (3½ x 15¾in)
- Three strips varying in width from 4–6cm (1½–2¼in)

From the third fat quarter cut

- Two short borders, 9 x 22cm (3½ x 8½in)
- Three or four strips varying in width from 4–6cm (1½–2¼in)
- 2.5cm (1in) wide bias-cut strips to cover piping cord, if you are making your own. Cut enough for 170cm (67in) of piping
- Interface all the border strips

How to make the pillow

1 Place your crazy patch right side up in the centre of the 22cm (8½in) square of wadding (batting). Place one strip, right side down, along one edge of the patch, matching the raw edges. Stitch with a 5mm (¼in) seam. Flip the strip over so that its right side is facing up, and trim to size. Place another strip along the next edge of the patch and the first strip, stitch, flip and trim. Continue around the crazy patch until the surface is completely covered. See page 22 for more details.

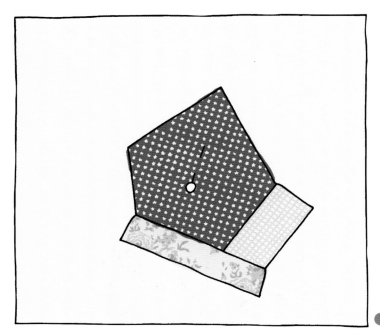

2 Turn the work over and trim the edges back to the size of the wadding (batting) to create a neat square.

3 Take the two short borders and stitch one to each side edge of the crazy patchwork panel, right sides together, taking a 5mm (¼in) seam. Open out the borders and press. Take the two long borders and stitch one to each remaining side edge, which includes the top/bottom of the short borders, again taking a 5mm (¼in) seam; press.

4 If you are not using a ready-made form of piping, now is the time to make your own: see page 36.

5 To add your piping, see pages 36–37 for more detail. Attach your zip foot. Starting in the middle of one pillow side, pin the piping to the pillow, right sides together, matching the raw edges, starting with the end that has been tucked inside the strip. Start stitching approximately 4cm (1¾in) from the beginning, stitching close to the piping cord. At the corner stop with the needle down, raise the presser foot, snip into the piping fabric, pivot and fold the piping along the next edge. Sew two to three stitches at an angle across the corner before pivoting and continuing along the next side. Repeat the process at the next corners.

6 As you approach the start of your stitching, stop with the needle down about 4cm (1½in) from the end. Raise the presser foot, unfold the piping strip at the beginning of your stitching and lay the end inside this fold, trimming the cord so that the ends meet. Refold the bias strip to encase the join in the cord, then continue stitching through all layers to the start of the stitching.

Tip

Use your stitch width button to move the needle when sewing a line of straight stitch in step 9. If you don't have a stitch width button, place the work so that the needle is to the left of your previous stitching and thus closer to the piping cord.

7 To create your pillow back, neaten one long edge of each back piece by taking a 1cm (½in) double hem: turn the edge under 1cm (½in), then again, to encase the raw edge. Top-stitch the hem in place. Press.

8 Lay the pillow front right side up on flat surface and place the pillow backs on top, right sides down, with all the outer edges matching – they will overlap in the centre at the hemmed edges. Pin around the edges, positioning the pins at right angles to the fabric. Turn the work over so that the pillow front is uppermost and you can see the previous row of stitching.

9 Move the needle position to the left of the previous stitching so that it is as close as possible to the piping. Sew all the way round. Attach the regular presser foot and stitch again with a zigzag stitch to neaten the raw edges. Trim close to the stitching, trimming the corners at an angle. Press and turn the cover through.

Baby playmat

86.5 x 86.5cm (34 x 34in)

This pretty playmat makes a perfect gift and gives you the chance to try
out your patchworking, quilting and appliqué skills.

YOU WILL NEED...

- Four fat quarters
- 92cm (36¼in) square of wadding (batting) and backing fabric
- Remnants of felt and fabric to create eight or nine appliqué shapes
- Paper-backed fusible web
- Interfacing to back the appliqué shapes
- Vanishing marking pen

Preparation

- Cut sixteen squares of 12.5 x 12.5cm (5 x 5in) from each of the fat quarters, making sixty-four squares in total

- Trace off the appliqué motifs (see pages 94–95), or draw your own. Fuse the paper-backed webbing to the reverse of your appliqué fabrics. Pin or draw around the appliqué motifs on the paper backing and when cool, cut out carefully. Remember, if you are using numbers or letters you need to draw them in reverse on the paper backing so that when turned over, they will be the right way round.

How to make the playmat

1 Peel the paper backing from the appliqué shapes and fuse them to the right sides of some of your cut squares. Using a vanishing marking pen, draw any details on the shapes that will be stitched, such as facial features.

2 Back these squares with interfacing and then stitch the motifs and details using your preferred appliqué method (see pages 38–39 for options). Here I used a mixture of free-motion stitching, blanket stitch, straight stitch and satin stitch.

3 With right sides together and taking a 5mm (¼in) seam allowance, sew two squares together along a side edge. Picking the squares at random, sew all the other squares together in pairs in the same way.

4 Now sew two pairs, right sides together, matching the seam in the centre of the pairs first, and then matching the top and bottom of the seam. Repeat until you have sewn all the pairs into square four-patches.

5 Sew two four-patches together, again matching the centre seam before lining up the top and bottom of the seam. Make sure that every eight-patch features one of your appliqué squares.

6 Join two eight-patches together at the sides to get a strip of eight across and two deep – make sure that you have only one appliqué each on the top and bottom rows. Repeat for the rest of the eight-patches so you have four sixteen-patch panels. Again, first pin at the centre seam, and then at the top and bottom of the seam.

7 Lay all the panels on a flat surface and decide which panel to join to which along the long edges. Once you have decided, take two adjacent panels and pin right sides together, pinning at the seams first to make sure all the squares match up. If you have one or two that don't match perfectly, match the seams, then clip two or three times into the seam allowance of the shorter one so that you can gently stretch it a little to make it fit. Sew the seam. Continue in this manner until all the panels are joined into one piece. Press all the seams.

Tip

Sew pair after pair together, leaving a small gap between pairs but without cutting the thread. This is known as chain piecing and is quicker than sewing all the pairs individually, and saves on thread.

8 Lay the backing fabric wrong side up on a flat surface. Add the wadding (batting) and then centre the pressed patchwork panel on top, right side up. The backing and wadding (batting) should extend approximately 2cm (¾in) beyond the panel. Anchor the layers together with pins, or by hand-basting (tacking), starting at the centre and working out to the edges, smoothing the layers as you go.

Tip
Baste (tack) with a contrast colour thread so that the stitches are easy to see and remove later.

9 Quilt the layers together: set your machine for free-motion stitching, attach the free-motion or darning foot and stitch all over the mat, except for the appliqué squares. I used a meandering stitch, but you could choose straight lines or stitch in the ditch.

10 If necessary, trim the wadding (batting) down close to the panel, and trim the backing so it is 2cm (¾in) larger than the panel. Press up a 1cm (½in) hem, then turn this over again by 1cm (½in) so that it wraps over the front edges of the patchwork by 1cm (½in).

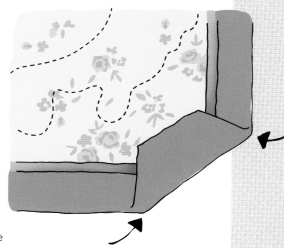

11 At the corners, unfold the double pressed edge, cut off the corner diagonally across where the first two fold lines cross. Fold the corner in along the second interlocking crease, then refold the edges so that the corner mitres neatly (see photograph, left). Pin in place.

12 Machine stitch around the edge, stitching close to the inner edge of the 'binding', using a stitch length of 3. To finish, hand stitch the diagonal fold of fabric at the corners.

Pretty pinafore

37 x 42cm (14½ x 16½in), excluding straps

Make your own little lady this pretty little pinafore, which can be worn in summer with a T-shirt or bare arms, or in winter with a sweater underneath.

How to make the pinafore

1 Fold the first fat quarter in half, right sides together, and lay it down in front of you with the short sides at the top and bottom. Cut armholes as follows: measure in 6cm (2¼in) from the outer edge along the top, mark. Measure down 10cm (4in) from the outer edges and mark. Join the two marks with a curved line to create the armholes. For the length – mark 44cm (17¼in) down from top edge and draw a horizontal line across bottom. Repeat for the second fat quarter.

2 To create the front of the dress: take one of the dress panels, turn under the top edge by 1cm (½in) then turn under by a further 4cm (1½in). Press and top-stitch close to the inner fold and again close to the edge. Find the centre of the top edge and mark with a pin.

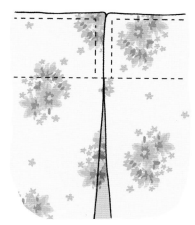

3 To create an inverted pleat, pin mark 5cm (2in) either side of centre pin mark, then fold the fabric at these outer pins and bring the fold to the centre to pleat. Pin in place. Stitch across the top along the previous stitching to hold the pleats in place. Also stitch down each pleat at the centre, as shown.

4 To create the back of the dress: turn under the top edge by 2.5cm (1in) twice and press. Top-stitch close to the edge and also close to the inner fold to create a casing for the elastic. Feed the elastic through the casing, and gather so that the back is 17cm (6¾in) wide when elasticated. Stitch the ends of the elastic in place at the sides to anchor.

5 Cut three rectangles of 25 x 15cm (10 x 6in). Fold two in half lengthways, with right sides together and press – these will be the straps. Fold the remaining one in half widthways and press. Cut this along the fold to create two smaller pieces – these will form your pocket. If desired, round off the bottom of the pocket pieces by folding in half lengthways and trimming the bottom edges in a curve.

6 Place the two pocket pieces right sides together and stitch around the edges, taking a 5mm (¼in) seam allowance and leaving a 5cm (2in) turning gap in one straight side edge. Clip the curves and corners at an angle and turn through, pushing out the curves and corners with a point turner or kebab stick. Press, tucking the raw edges of the opening inside.

7 Top-stitch across the pocket top, 1cm (½in) from the edge. Then fold the pocket piece in half lengthways and stitch 5mm (¼in) from the fold down 15mm (⅝in) to create a little pleat.

8 Position the pocket on the dress front and edge stitch in place, closing the turning gap as you go.

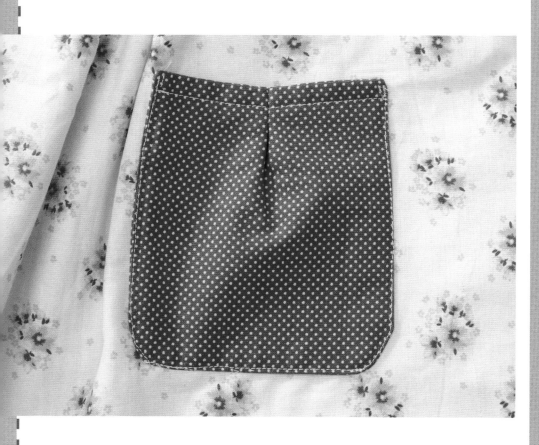

9 Stitch the folded strap pieces down one long edge and turn through, refolding so the seam is in the centre. Tuck the raw ends inside, press and stitch.

10 Pin the straps to the wrong side of the dress back, 1cm (½in) from the side edge and with the seam of the strap on the underside and the bottom of the strap just below the casing. Stitch in place, stitching over the casing stitching. Stitch again from the right side, along the top edge of the dress, again along the previous row of stitching.

11 The side seams of the dress are French seams (see page 19). Sew the side seams, wrong sides together with a 5mm (¼in) seam allowance. Trim to 3mm (⅛in) and turn through; press with the seam on the edge. Stitch again, right sides together, with a 1cm (½in) seam allowance; press.

12 Next you will create your binding. Cut two strips of the contrast fabric 23cm x 3.5cm (9 x 1⅜in). Fold one long edge under by 5mm (¼in) and press. Fold the short ends of the binding to the wrong side and press. Pin the long, unfolded edge to the wrong side of the armhole with raw edges aligned. Stitch, taking a 1cm (½in) seam allowance. Flip the binding over to the right side of the dress, pin and stitch close to the binding edge. Finish the ends by hand. Repeat for the other armhole.

13 To add some detail to the front of the straps, fold them in half lengthways, right sides together and stitch 1cm (½in) from the fold for 7cm (2¾in) to create a pleat.

14 Make a vertical buttonhole on each side of the top of the dress, 2.5cm (1in) in from the edge.

15 Try the dress on and then attach buttons to the front of the straps at the required position.

16 Turn up a double hem, turning under 1cm (½in) and then again another 1cm (½in) to encase the raw edge. Top-stitch in place.

Templates

All the templates given here are shown at actual size – simply trace them off and use them. Remember, when drawing numbers or letters on to your paper backing for appliqué, you will need to use them back to front, so that they are correct when cut out.

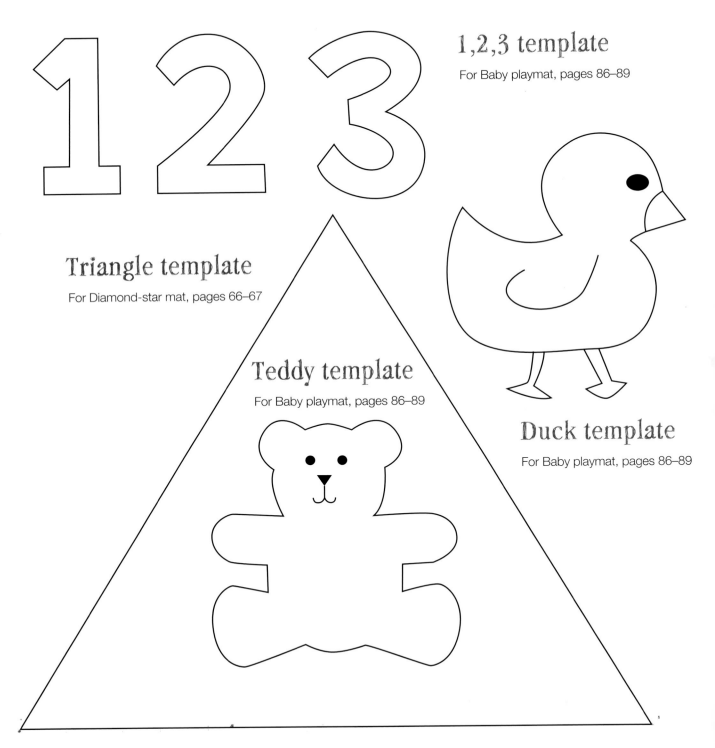

1,2,3 template

For Baby playmat, pages 86–89

Triangle template

For Diamond-star mat, pages 66–67

Teddy template

For Baby playmat, pages 86–89

Duck template

For Baby playmat, pages 86–89

Elephant, cat, dog, star, car and beach hut templates

For Baby playmat, pages 86–89

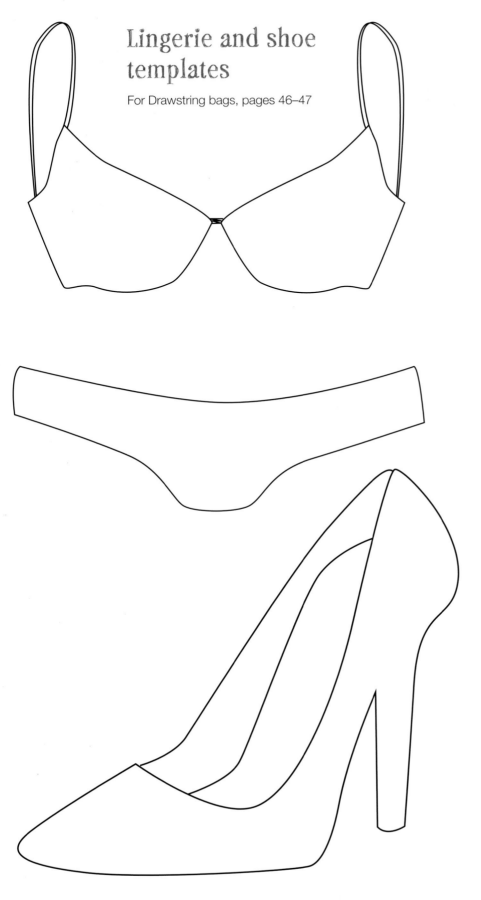

Lingerie and shoe templates

For Drawstring bags, pages 46–47

Index